KT-367-849

Willy Russell

Blood Brothers

BLOOMSBURY

LONDON • NEW DELHI • NEW YORK • SYDNEY

Bloomsbury Methuen Drama
An imprint of Bloomsbury Publishing Plc

50 Bedford Square   1385 Broadway
London   New York
WC1B 3DP   NY 10018
UK   USA

www.bloomsbury.com

First published in a collection with *Educating Rita* and
Stags and Hens in 1986 by Methuen Drama
This edition first published in Great Britain in 2001
by Methuen Publishing Limited
Reissued with a new cover design by Bloomsbury Methuen Drama 2009
Reprinted 2010 (twice), 2011, 2012, 2013

Copyright © 1985 by Willy Russell

Willy Russell has asserted his right under the Copyright, Designs and
Patents Act, 1988, to be identified as author of this work.

All rights reserved. No part of this publication may be reproduced or transmitted in
any form or by any means, electronic or mechanical, including photocopying,
recording, or any information storage or retrieval system, without prior
permission in writing from the publishers.

No responsibility for loss caused to any individual or organization acting on or
refraining from action as a result of the material in this publication
can be accepted by Bloomsbury or the author.

All rights whatsoever in this play are strictly reserved and application for
performance etc. should be made before rehearsals by professionals and
by amateurs to Casarotto Ramsay and

Associates Limited, Waverley House, 7–12 Noel Street, London WIF 8GQ. No
performance may be given unless a licence has been obtained.

No rights in incidental music or songs contained in the work are hereby granted
and performance rights for any performance/presentation whatsoever must be
obtained from the respective copyright owners.

Visit www.bloomsbury.com to find out more about our authors and their books
You will find extracts, author interviews, author events and you can sign up for
newsletters to be the first to hear about our latest releases and special offers.

British Library Cataloguing-in-Publication Data
A catalogue record for this book is available from the British Library.

ISBN: PB: 978-0-4137-6770-7
ePDF: 978-1-4081-1536-7
ePub: 978-1-4725-3638-9

Library of Congress Cataloging-in-Publication Data
A catalog record for this book is available from the Library of Congress.

Typeset by Country Setting, Kingsdown, Kent
Printed and bound in India

Methuen Drama Modern Classics

The Methuen Drama Modern Plays series has always been at
the forefront of modern playwriting and has reflected the most
exciting developments in modern drama since 1959. To
commemorate the fiftieth anniversary of Methuen Drama, the
series was relaunched in 2009 as Methuen Drama Modern
Classics, and continues to offer readers a choice selection of
the best modern plays.

Blood Brothers

'*Blood Brothers* is undoubtedly the most exciting thing to have
happened to the English musical theatre in years . . . essentially
a folk opera, a Liverpudlian *West Side Story*, about twin brothers
who grow up on opposite sides of the social tracks without
realising their fraternity.'   Sheridan Morley

'Willy Russell is less concerned with political tub-thumping
than with weaving a close-knit story about the working of fate
and destiny . . . it carries one along with it in almost
unreserved enjoyment.'   *Guardian*

Willy Russell was born in Whiston, near Liverpool. Leaving
school at fifteen, he worked variously as a ladies' hairdresser,
warehouseman and girder cleaner until, at the age of twenty-
one, he returned to education. It was while training to become
a teacher that he wrote his first plays for both stage and
television. *Playground*, *Keep Your Eyes Down* and *Sam O'Shanker*
were premiered at St Katherine's College in 1972. Under the
collective title *Blind Scouse* these were presented later the same
year at the Edinburgh Festival Fringe, where they were seen by
playwright John McGrath and led to Russell writing *When the
Reds*, adapted from an original script by Alan Plater, for the
Everyman Theatre, Liverpool (1973). Subsequently he has
written *John Paul George Ringo . . . and Bert* (Everyman and Lyric,

London, 1974; winner of the *Evening Standard* and London
Theatre Critics' Awards for Best Musical), *Breezeblock Park*
(Everyman, 1975; Mermaid and Whitehall, London, 1977), *One
for the Road* (Contact Theatre, Manchester, 1976; Lyric,
London, 1987), *Stags and Hens* (Everyman, 1978; Young Vic,
1983; revised and presented as *Stags and Hens – The Remix*, Royal
Court, Liverpool, 2008), *Educating Rita* (RSC Warehouse and
Piccadilly, London, 1980, winner of SWET Best Comedy
Award), *Blood Brothers* (play version, Merseyside Young People's
Theatre Company, 1981), *Blood Brothers* (musical version,
Liverpool Playhouse and Lyric, London, 1983; Albery and
Phoenix, London, 1988; Music Box, New York, 1993), *Our Day
Out* (play version, Everyman and Young Vic, 1983; musical
version, Royal Court, Liverpool, 2009), *Shirley Valentine*
(Everyman, 1986; Vaudeville, London, 1988, winner of Olivier
Award for Best Comedy; Booth Theatre, New York, 1989).

For television he has written *King of the Castle* (BBC, 1973),
Break-In (BBC, 1974), *Death of a Young Young Man* (BBC, 1974),
Our Day Out (BBC, 1976), *Lies* (BBC, 1978), *The Daughters of
Albion* (ITV, 1979), *Politics and Terror* (ITV, 1980), *The Boy with the
Transistor Radio* (ITV, 1980), the *One Summer* series (Channel 4,
1983), *Terraces* (BBC, 1993). Feature films and screenplays
include *Educating Rita* (winner of *Evening Standard* Award for Best
Screenplay, 1983), *Shirley Valentine* (1989), *Dancin' Thru the Dark*
(1990), *Blood Brothers* (with Alan Parker, 2006). As a composer
Russell has written for the TV series *Connie* and the feature film
Mr Love, as well as for his own films, *Shirley Valentine* and *Dancin'
Thru the Dark*. He wrote music and lyrics for *Blood Brothers* and
(with Bob Eaton and Chris Mellor) music and lyrics for *Our
Day Out*. With the poets Adrian Henri, Brian Patten and Roger
McGough, he wrote and performed *Words on the Run* (1995–7),
and with playwright Tim Firth he wrote and performed *In Other
Words* (2004) and *The Singing Playwrights* (2004). In 2003 he wrote
and recorded the CD *Hoovering the Moon*. His novel *The Wrong
Boy* was published by Doubleday in 2000.

I Want to Write a Musical

For years I'd wanted to write a musical. Not the book of a musical or even the lyrics and the book. I wanted to write a musical – book, lyrics *and* the music. Now there's cheek! Book? Well, yes. Lyrics? Possibly. But the music? I could quite understand the objections, the pitying looks of disbelief. I'd got no record of writing music for the theatre and I had to admit that yes, it's quite true, during my schooldays a succession of music teachers had contributed to my annual reports comments such as: 'Shows absolutely no interest', 'If he continues with this subject next year I will be forced to tender my resignation', 'We will consider it an achievement if he learns to play the gramophone'.

No wonder that years and years later when asked casually at parties or in bars what I was working on, the reply, 'A musical', would invariably provoke the response, 'Ah. And who's writing the music?'

Feebly, apologetically I'd whisper, 'Me.' 'Pardon?'

'Me', just as feeble, inaudible. A cough and the word repeated, unintentionally loud, 'ME . . . me.'

And as the other party would nod a sickly, sympathetic nod and break away with cries of 'Oh, there's Alan, I haven't seen Alan for weeks', I'd seize his arm and begin my speech about 'But oh, look, I mean it will be all right. I mean, I can write music, honest, I wrote music and songs for years and years before I became a playwright and I mean, I know no one knows about my music but if you'd been around in the days of the Green Moose when I used to write ten, twelve songs a week! Take no notice of what those daft music teachers said, cos they didn't know that while they were screamin' about my failure to appreciate "Dashin' Away with the Smoothin' Iron" or some stupid bloody song about ripe cherries, I was secretly, secretly goin' round to Roger Rimmer's house where we had two guitars an' where we'd stand in front of the mirror for hours pretendin' to be the Shadows! So there.'

By which time, of course, I was talking to no one but myself. Which is as it should have been because I really had no one to convince other than myself. It was true, I had for many years,

before I'd ever put a foot inside a theatre, written and performed
hundreds of songs. I clutched onto this historical fact like a
drowning man clutching at a floating crisp packet. I might have
written hundreds of songs but I couldn't ignore the fact that
every single one of them was quite unknown. Even the few that
were recorded passed, quite unnoticed, into the oblivion of
instant deletions.

And *I* want to write a musical, am indeed, somewhere in the
middle of it, when my wise and crazy agent, after listening to
my passionate I've-been-writing-songs-for-years speech, fixes me
with her fork and says, 'Yes, dear boy, but this is the theatre,
and in the musical theatre you must, absolutely *must* be
hummable. To not be hummable in the musical theatre is
nothing less than treason! Well, dear?'

'What?'

'Are you? Hummable?'

All the way back on the train, staring glumly into the night,
even failing to notice for once that feller who's always trying to
get to Glasgow but always ends up on the Liverpool train and
always slumps in the seat opposite me, and always tells me he's
the ex-karate champion of Greenock and if I want a fight,
he's my man although he's currently one of Glasgow's leading
industrialists but could I see my way to buy him a wee can of
lager. Or two . . .

I am not hummable!

The woman with the two kids on the seat across the aisle
begins to hum a melody to get the baby to sleep. I surreptiti-
ously lean across, discreetly trying to hear what she is humming,
in the desperate hope that years ago she might have been in the
audience in the Green Moose, that she might be humming one
of my . . . I hear the unmistakably hummable strains of
'Memories' and groan audibly as the baby sits bolt upright and
accuses me of being its 'dada, dada . . . dada'.

My old friend from Glasgow attempts to fix me with a glare
and, addressing a space six inches to the side of my head, tells
me I should make a respectable woman out of her. He's
distracted by the outraged mother and the kids, who are now
both crying, and he offers to sing them to sleep. The mother
protests and it's not a spectacle I wish to promote but supposing,

I mean you never know, he might have been at the Green
Moose . . . Hopes dashed as he launches into a cross between
'Mull of Kintyre' and 'My Way'.

That night, a nightmare consisting of a million snippets from
likely reviews, one in particular ringing in my ears as I wake,
bathed in sweat:

'It is plain that the composer does not know a crotchet from
a hatchet though I would readily concede that armed with a
hatchet Mr Russell could do no worse damage than he can with
a crotchet.'

In the morning, bog-eyed and trembling, staggering down to
the kitchen to find the kids already up, dressed for school,
attacking Coco-Pops and each other. Filling the kettle, pro-
viding the morning arbitration service, trying to apply futile
liberal ideals to the kids' uncomplicated straightforward
brutality: 'That's mine', 'No it's not', 'Well, I'm not gonna be
your friend, ever!', SCREAMS, 'Dad, Dad, she's got my Star
Wars figure an' I'm gonna take her Sindy Doll cos that's fair an'
I'm gonna break it!' A normal sort of morning, something like
a session at the United Nations, with breakfast cereal. And
through it all, inside, I'm composing my defence speech for when
I come to stand in the Court of Musical Crimes, accused of
TRYING TO WRITE A MUSICAL, facing a jury which
includes the Gershwins, Mr Sondheim, Kern, Porter, Mr
Rodgers and Mr Lloyd Webber and all their collaborators. I
hardly notice that the kids have signed the day's first ceasefire,
that they're ready and on their way out to school, that I've
given them the wrong packed lunch or the right dinner money,
PE pumps, swimming costumes and contributions to the
school's Better Housing for Hamsters Fund. Hardly notice
anything. Hardly notice that through all this Ruthie has been
humming some dimly recognisable melody,

We've kissed goodbye, I've watched them set off on the short
walk to school, I've got a cup of tea and a ciggy and I'm slumped
in the kitchen chair exhausted. And it's a full ten minutes before
I realise what the melody was. I'm out of the door and running
wildly towards the school. I catch up with her in the playground
and she's surprised and slightly startled and even amused that
Dad should be in the playground wearing slippers.

'Quickly,' I say, 'just quickly hum me a few bars of that tune.' And suddenly I'm jumping up and down in the playground, shrieking with delight, because from only the briefest of hearings one of my kids has picked up a melody of mine. I'm shouting 'Hummable, hummable', over and over again. Ruthie's beaming at me, asking me if I want to play hopscotch as well. Other kids are looking at me as though I'm a fully-fledged nut and teachers are streaming from all directions to apprehend a man gone mad.

After satisfying the headmaster that I'm a mere parent suffering from nothing more dangerous than Chronic-Desire-to-Write-a-Musical, he instructs the caretaker and the peri-patetic music teacher to release their grip on me, lectures me about a playground being no place to behave like a child and has me escorted from the grounds. I walk down Church Road, elated, seeing clearly the green of the trees, the yellow of the sunlight.

And I know I can go on – because Ruthie was humming one of my tunes.

About a year later, *Blood Brothers* having opened, audiences and critics having responded more kindly than they had in my dreams, I was driving to Wales with the family. The car radio was playing and a song from *Blood Brothers* was introduced. I reached across to turn up the volume when from the back of the car a small voice said, 'Oh not that bloody song again.' I went to say: 'Ruthie! Don't swear.' But fair's fair. I slipped in a cassette of her favourite nursery rhymes and we carried on to Wales singing 'Lavender's Blue' and 'Cock-a-Doodle-Doo'.

Willy Russell

Blood Brothers

Production note

The setting for *Blood Brothers* is an open stage, with the different settings and time spans being indicated by lighting changes, with the minimum of properties and furniture. The whole play should flow along easily and smoothly, with no cumbersome scene changes. Two areas are semi-permanent – the Lyons house and the Johnstone house. We see the interior of the Lyonses' comfortable home but usually only the exterior front door of the Johnstone house, with the 'interior' scenes taking place outside the door. The area between the two houses acts as communal ground for street scenes, park scenes, etc.

Blood Brothers was first performed at the Liverpool Playhouse on 8 January 1983, with the following cast:

Mrs Johnstone	Barbara Dickson
Mickey	George Costigan
Edward	Andrew C. Wadsworth
Sammy	Peter Christian
Linda	Amanda York
Mrs Lyons	Wendy Murray
Mr Lyons	Alan Leith
Narrator	Andrew Schofield
Chorus	Hazel Ellerby, Eithne Brown, David Edge

Directed by Chris Bond
Designed by Andy Greenfield
Musical Director Peter Filleul

Blood Brothers was subsequently presented by Bob Swash, by arrangement with Liverpool Playhouse, at the Lyric Theatre, London, on 11 April 1983, with the following cast:

Mrs Johnstone	Barbara Dickson
Mickey	George Costigan
Edward	Andrew C. Wadsworth
Sammy	Peter Christian
Linda	Kate Fitzgerald
Mrs Lyons	Wendy Murray
Mr Lyons	Alan Leith
Narrator	Andrew Schofield
Chorus	Hazel Ellerby, David Edge, Ian Burns, Oliver Beamish

Directed by Chris Bond and Danny Hiller
Designed by Andy Greenfield
Musical Director Richard Spanswick

Characters

Mrs Johnstone
Mickey
Edward
Sammy
Linda
Mrs Lyons
Mr Lyons
Narrator
Chorus

Act One

The overture comes to a close.

Mrs Johnstone (*singing*)
  Tell me it's not true. Say it's just a story.

The **Narrator** *steps forward.*

Narrator (*speaking*)
  So did y' hear the story of the Johnstone twins?
  As like each other as two new pins,
  Of one womb born, on the selfsame day,
  How one was kept and one given away?
  An' did you never hear how the Johnstones died,
  Never knowing that they shared one name,
  Till the day they died, when a mother cried
  My own dear sons lie slain?

The lights come up to show a re-enactment of the final moments of the play – the deaths of **Mickey** *and* **Edward**. *The scene fades.*

Mrs Johnstone *enters with her back to the audience.*

Narrator
  An' did y' never hear of the mother, so cruel,
  There's a stone in place of her heart?
  Then bring her on and come judge for yourselves
  How she came to play this part.

The **Narrator** *exits.*

Music is heard as **Mrs Johnstone** *turns and walks towards us. She is aged thirty but looks more like fifty.*

Mrs Johnstone (*singing*)
  Once I had a husband,
  You know the sort of chap,
  I met him at a dance and how he came on with the chat.
  He said my eyes were deep blue pools,
  My skin as soft as snow,
  He told me I was sexier than Marilyn Monroe.

And we went dancing,
We went dancing.

Then, of course, I found
That I was six weeks overdue.
We got married at the registry an' then we had a 'do'.
We all had curly salmon sandwiches,
An' how the ale did flow,
They said the bride was lovelier than Marilyn Monroe.

And we went dancing,
Yes, we went dancing.

Then the baby came along,
We called him Darren Wayne,
Then three months on I found that I was in the club again.
An' though I still fancied dancing,
My husband wouldn't go,
With a wife he said was twice the size of Marilyn Monroe.

No more dancing
No more dancing.

By the time I was twenty-five,
I looked like forty-two,
With seven hungry mouths to feed and one more nearly due.
Me husband, he'd walked out on me,
A month or two ago,
For a girl they say who looks a bit like Marilyn Monroe.

And they go dancing
They go dancing

Yes they go dancing
They go . . .

An irate **Milkman** (*the* **Narrator**) *rushes in to rudely interrupt the song.*

Milkman   Listen, love, I'm up to here with hard-luck stories; you own me three pounds, seventeen and fourpence an' either you pay up today, like now, or I'll be forced to cut off your deliveries.

Mrs Johnstone   I said, I said, look, next week I'll pay y' –

Milkman   Next week, next week! Next week never arrives around here. I'd be a rich man if next week ever came.

Mrs Johnstone   But look, look, I start a job next week. I'll have money comin' in an' I'll be able to pay y'. Y' can't stop the milk. I need the milk. I'm pregnant.

Milkman   Well, don't look at me, love. I might be a milkman but it's got nothin' to do with me. Now you've been told, no money, no milk.

The **Milkman** *exits.*

Mrs Johnstone *stands alone and we hear some other kids, off.*

Kid One *(off)*   Mam, Mam, the baby's cryin'. He wants his bottle. Where's the milk?

Kid Two *(off)*   'Ey, Mam, how come I'm on free dinners? All the other kids laugh at me.

Kid Three *(off)*   'Ey, Mother, I'm starvin' an' there's nothin' in. There never bloody well is.

Mrs Johnstone *(perfunctorily)*   Don't swear, I've told y'.

Kid Four *(off)*   Mum, I can't sleep, I'm hungry, I'm starvin' . . .

Kids *(off)*   An' me, Mam. An' me. An' me.

Mrs Johnstone *(singing)*
  I know it's hard on all you kids,
  But try and get some sleep.
  Next week I'll be earnin',
  We'll have loads of things to eat,
  We'll have ham, an' jam, an' spam an'
  (Speaking.) Roast Beef, Yorkshire Puddin', Battenberg Cake,
  Chicken an' Chips, Corned Beef, Sausages, Treacle Tart,
  Mince an' Spuds, Milk Shake for the Baby.

There is a chorus of groaning ecstasy from the **Kids**.

Mrs Johnstone *(picks up the tune again)*
  When I bring home the dough,
  We'll live like kings, like bright young things,

Like Marilyn Monroe.
And we'll go dancing . . .

Mrs Johnstone *hums a few bars of the song, and dances a few steps, as she makes her way to her place of work –* **Mrs Lyons***'s house. During the dance she acquires a brush, dusters and a mop bucket.*

Mrs Lyons*'s house, where* **Mrs Johnstone** *is working.* **Mrs Lyons** *enters carrying a parcel.*

Mrs Lyons   Hello, Mrs Johnstone, how are you? Is the job working out all right for you?

Mrs Johnstone   It's, erm, great. Thank you. It's such a lovely house it's a pleasure to clean it.

Mrs Lyons   It's a pretty house, isn't it? It's a pity it's so big. I'm finding it rather large at present.

Mrs Johnstone   Oh. Yeh. With Mr Lyons being away an' that? When does he come back, Mrs Lyons?

Mrs Lyons   Oh, it seems such a long time. The Company sent him out there for nine months, so, what's that, he'll be back in about five months' time.

Mrs Johnstone   Ah, you'll be glad when he's back, won't you? The house won't feel so empty then, will it?

Mrs Lyons *begins to unwrap her parcel.*

Mrs Lyons   Actually, Mrs J, we bought such a large house for the – for the children – we thought children would come along.

Mrs Johnstone   Well, y' might still be able to . . .

Mrs Lyons   No, I'm afraid . . . We've been trying for such a long time now . . . I wanted to adopt but . . . Mr Lyons is . . . well, he says he wanted his own son, not someone else's. Myself, I believe that an adopted child can become one's own.

Mrs Johnstone   Ah yeh . . . yeh. 'Ey, it's weird though, isn't it? Here's you can't have kids, an' me, I can't stop havin' them. Me husband used to say that all we had to do was shake hands and I'd be in the club. He must have shook hands with me before he left. I'm havin' another one, y' know.

Mrs Lyons   Oh, I see . . .

Mrs Johnstone   Oh but look, look, it's all right, Mrs Lyons, I'll still be able to do me work. Havin' babies, it's like clockwork to me. I'm back on me feet an' workin' the next day, y' know. If I have this one at the weekend I won't even need to take one day off. I love this job, y' know. We can just manage to get by now —

She is stopped by **Mrs Lyons** *putting the contents of the package, a pair of new shoes, on to the table.*

Mrs Johnstone   Jesus Christ, Mrs Lyons, what are y' trying to do?

Mrs Lyons   My God, what's wrong?

Mrs Johnstone   The shoes . . . the shoes . . .

Mrs Lyons   Pardon?

Mrs Johnstone   New shoes on the table, take them off . . .

Mrs Lyons *does so.*

Mrs Johnstone (*relieved*)   Oh God, Mrs Lyons, never put new shoes on a table . . . You never know what'll happen.

Mrs Lyons (*twigging it; laughing*)   Oh . . . you mean you're superstitious?

Mrs Johnstone   No, but you never put new shoes on the table.

Mrs Lyons   Oh, go on with you. Look, if it will make you any happier I'll put them away.

She exits with the shoes.

Music is heard as **Mrs Johnstone** *warily approaches the table and the* **Narrator** *enters.*

Narrator   There's shoes upon the table an' a joker in the pack. The salt's been spilled and a looking glass cracked. There's one lone magpie overhead.

Mrs Johnstone   I'm not superstitious.

Narrator   The Mother said.

Mrs Johnstone   I'm not superstitious.

Narrator The Mother said.

The **Narrator** *exits to re-enter as a* **Gynaecologist**.

Mrs Johnstone   What are you doin' here? The milk bill's not due till Thursday.

Gynaecologist (*producing a listening funnel*)   Actually I've given up the milk round and gone into medicine. I'm your gynaecologist. (*He begins to examine her.*) OK, Mummy, let's have a little listen to the baby's ticker, shall we?

Mrs Johnstone   I was dead worried about havin' another baby, you know, Doctor. I didn't see how we were gonna manage with another mouth to feed. But now I've got me a little job we'll be OK. If I'm careful we can just scrape by, even with another mouth to feed.

The **Gynaecologist** *completes his examination.*

Gynaecologist   Mouths, Mummy.

Mrs Johnstone   What?

Gynaecologist   Plural, Mrs Johnstone. Mouths to feed. You're expecting twins. Congratulations. And the next one please, Nurse.

The **Gynaecologist** *exits.*

Mrs Johnstone, *numbed by the news, moves back to her work, dusting the table upon which the shoes had been placed.*

Mrs Lyons *enters.*

Mrs Lyons   Hello, Mrs J. How are you?

There is no reply.

(*Registering the silence.*) Mrs J? Anything wrong?

Mrs Johnstone   I had it all worked out.

Mrs Lyons   What's the matter?

Mrs Johnstone   We were just getting straight.

Mrs Lyons   Why don't you sit down.

Mrs Johnstone   With one more baby we could have managed. But not with two. The welfare have already been on to me. They say I'm incapable of controllin' the kids I've already got. They say I should put some of them into care. But I won't. I love the bones of every one of them. I'll even love these two when they come along. But like they say at the welfare, kids can't live on love alone.

Mrs Lyons   Twins? You're expecting twins?

The **Narrator** *enters.*

Narrator
How quickly an idea, planted, can
Take root and grow into a plan.
The thought conceived in this very room
Grew as surely as a seed, in a mother's womb.

The **Narrator** *exits.*

Mrs Lyons (*almost inaudibly*)   Give one to me.

Mrs Johnstone   What?

Mrs Lyons (*containing her excitement*)   Give one of them to me.

Mrs Johnstone   Give one to you?

Mrs Lyons   Yes . . . yes.

Mrs Johnstone (*taking it almost as a joke*)   But y' can't just . . .

Mrs Lyons   When are you due?

Mrs Johnstone   Erm, well, about . . . Oh, but Mrs . . .

Mrs Lyons   Quickly, quickly, tell me . . . when are you due?

Mrs Johnstone   July he said, the beginning of . . .

Mrs Lyons   July . . . and my husband doesn't get back until the middle of July. He need never guess . . .

Mrs Johnstone (*amused*)   Oh, it's mad . . .

Mrs Lyons   I know, it is. It's mad . . . but it's wonderful, it's perfect. Look, look, you're what, four months pregnant, but you're only just beginning to show . . . so, so I'm four months pregnant and I'm only just beginning to show. (*She grabs a cushion and arranges it beneath her dress.*) Look, look. I could have got pregnant just before he went away. But I didn't tell him in case I miscarried, I didn't want to worry him whilst he was away. But when he arrives home I tell him we were wrong, the doctors werc wrong. I have a baby, our baby. Mrs Johnstone, it will work, it will if only you'll . . .

Mrs Johnstone   Oh, Mrs Lyons, you can't be serious.

Mrs Lyons   You said yourself, you said you had too many children already.

Mrs Johnstone   Yeh, but I don't know if I wanna give one away.

Mrs Lyons   Already you're being threatened by the welfare people. Mrs Johnstone, with two more children how can you possibly avoid some of them being put into care? Surely, it's better to give one child to me. Look, at least if the child was with me you'd be able to see him every day, as you came to work.

She stares at **Mrs Johnstone***, willing her to agree.*

Mrs Lyons   Please, Mrs Johnstone. Please.

Mrs Johnstone   Are y' . . . are y' that desperate to have a baby?

Mrs Lyons (*singing*)
Each day I look out from this window,
I see him with his friends, I hear him call,
I rush down but as I fold my arms around him,
He's gone. Was he ever there at all?
I've dreamed of all the places I would take him,
The games we'd play, the stories I would tell,

The jokes we'd share, the clothing I would make him,
I reach out. But as I do. He fades away.

The melody shifts into that of **Mrs Johnstone** *who is looking at*
Mrs Lyons, *feeling for her.* **Mrs Lyons** *gives her a half-smile and a*
shrug, perhaps slightly embarrassed at what she has revealed. **Mrs**
Johnstone *turns and looks at the room she is in. Looking up in awe at*
the comparative opulence and ease of the place. Tentatively and wondering
she sings:

Mrs Johnstone
If my child was raised
In a palace like this one,
(He) wouldn't have to worry where
His next meal was comin' from.
His clothing would be (supplied by)
George Henry Lee.

Mrs Lyons *sees that* **Mrs Johnstone** *might be persuaded.*

Mrs Lyons (*singing*)
He'd have all his own toys
And a garden to play in.

Mrs Johnstone
He could make too much noise
Without the neighbours complainin'.

Mrs Lyons
Silver trays to take meals on.

Mrs Johnstone
A bike with *both* wheels on?

Mrs Lyons *nods enthusiastically.*

Mrs Lyons
And he'd sleep every night
In a bed of his own.

Mrs Johnstone
He wouldn't get into fights
He'd leave matches alone.
And you'd never find him

Effin' and blindin'.
And when he grew up
He could never be told
To stand and queue up
For hours on end at the dole
He'd grow up to be

Mrs Lyons *and* **Mrs Johnstone** (*together*)
A credit to me.

Mrs Johnstone
To you.

I would still be able to see him every day, wouldn't I?

Mrs Lyons   Of course.

Mrs Johnstone   An' . . . an' you would look after him, wouldn't y'?

Mrs Lyons (*singing*)
I'd keep him warm in the winter
And cool when it shines.
I'd pull out his splinters
Without making him cry.
I'd always be there
If his dream was a nightmare.
My child.
My child.

There is a pause before **Mrs Johnstone** *nods.* **Mrs Lyons** *goes across and kisses her, hugs her.* **Mrs Johnstone** *is slightly embarrassed.*

Mrs Lyons   Oh. Now you must help me. There's so much . . . I'll have to . . . (*She takes out the cushion.*) We'll do this properly so that it's thoroughly convincing, and I'll need to see you walk, and baby clothes, I'll have to knit and buy bottles and suffer from piles.

Mrs Johnstone   What?

Mrs Lyons   Doesn't one get piles when one's pregnant? And buy a cot and . . . Oh, help me with this, Mrs J. Is it in the right place? (*She puts the cushion back again.*) I want it to look right before I go shopping.

Mrs Johnstone (*helping her with the false pregnancy*)   What you goin' the shops for? I do the shopping.

Mrs Lyons   Oh no, from now on I do the shopping. I want everyone to know about my baby. (*She suddenly reaches for the Bible.*)

Music.

Mrs J, we must make this a, erm, a binding agreement.

Mrs Lyons *shows the Bible to* **Mrs Johnstone**, *who is at first reluctant and then lays her hand on it.*

The **Narrator** *enters. A bass note, repeated as a heartbeat.*

Narrator
In the name of Jesus, the thing was done,
Now there's no going back, for anyone.
It's too late now, for feeling torn
There's a pact been sealed, there's a deal been born.

Mrs Lyons *puts the Bible away.* **Mrs Johnstone** *stands and stares as* **Mrs Lyons**, *grabs shopping bags and takes a last satisfied glance at herself in the mirror.*

Mrs Johnstone   Why . . . why did we have to do that?

Mrs Lyons   Mrs J, nobody must ever know. Therefore we have to have an agreement.

Mrs Johnstone *nods but is still uncomfortable.*

Mrs Lyons   Right, I shan't be long. Bye.

Mrs Lyons *exits.*

Mrs Johnstone *stands alone, afraid.*

The heartbeat grows in intensity.

Narrator
How swiftly those who've made a pact,
Can come to overlook the fact.

> Or wish the reckoning to be delayed
> But a debt is a debt, and must be paid.

The **Narrator** *exits.*

As the heartbeat reaches maximum volume it suddenly stops and is replaced by the sound of crying babies.

Two nurses appear, each carrying a bundle. A pram is wheeled on.

The nurses hand the bundles to **Mrs Johnstone** *who, smiling, places them into the pram. Making faces and noises at the babies she stops the crying. The babies settled, she sets off, wheeling the pram towards home.*

Various debt collectors emerge from her house to confront **Mrs Johnstone**.

Catalogue Man   I'm sorry, love . . . the kids said you were at the hospital. (*He looks into the pram.*) Ah . . . they're lovely, aren't they? I'm sorry, love, especially at a time like this, but, you are twelve weeks behind in your payments. I've got to do this, girl . . .

Finance Man   Y' shouldn't sign for the bloody stuff, missis. If y' know y' can't pay, y' shouldn't bloody well sign.

Catalogue Man   Look, if y' could give me a couple of weeks' money on this I could leave it.

Mrs Johnstone *shakes her head.*

Finance Man   Y' shouldn't have signed for all this stuff, should y'? Y' knew y' wouldn't be able to pay, didn't y'?

Mrs Johnstone (*almost to herself*)   When I got me job, I thought I would be able to pay. When I went in the showroom I only meant to come out with a couple of things. But when you're standing there, it all looks so nice. When y' look in the catalogue an' there's six months to pay, it seems years away, an' y' need a few things so y' sign.

Finance Man   Yeh, well, y' bloody well shouldn't.

Mrs Johnstone (*coming out of her trance; angrily*)   I know I shouldn't, you soft get. I've spent all me bleedin' life knowin' I *shouldn't*. But I do. Now, take y' soddin' wireless and get off.

Catalogue Man   Ah well, as long as y' can laugh about it, eh, that's the main thing, isn't it?

The **Catalogue Man** *exits.*

Mrs Johnstone (*not laughing*)   Yeh.

Other creditors continue to enter the house and leave with goods.

Mrs Johnstone *watches the creditors. The babies begin to cry and she moves to the pram, rocking it gently as she sings, as if to the babies in the pram.*

Mrs Johnstone (*singing*)
     Only mine until
     The time comes round
     To pay the bill.
     Then, I'm afraid,
     What can't be paid
     Must be returned.
     You never, ever learn,
     That nothing's yours,
     On easy terms.

     Only for a time,
     I must not learn,
     To call you mine.
     Familiarise
     That face, those eyes
     Make future plans
     That cannot be confirmed.
     On borrowed time,
     On easy terms.

     Living on the never never,
     Constant as the changing weather,
     Never sure
     Who's at the door
     Or the price I'll have to pay.

Should we meet again
I will not recognise your name.
You can be sure
What's gone before
Will be concealed.
Your friends will never learn
That once we were
On easy terms.

Living on the never never,
Constant as the changing weather,
Never sure
Who's at the door
Or the price I'll have to pay . . .

Mrs Lyons *enters, still with the pregnancy padding.*

Mrs Lyons   They're born, you didn't notify me.

Mrs Johnstone   Well, I . . . I just . . . it's . . . couldn't I keep
them for a few more days, please, please, they're a pair, they go
together.

Mrs Lyons   My husband is due back tomorrow, Mrs
Johnstone. I must have my baby. We made an agreement, a
bargain. You swore on the Bible.

Mrs Johnstone   You'd better . . . you'd better see which one
you want.

Mrs Lyons   I'll take . . .

Mrs Johnstone   No. Don't tell me which one. Just take him,
take him.

(*Singing*) Living on the never never,
Constant as the changing weather,
Never sure
Who's at the door
Or the price I'll have to pay,
Should we meet again . . .

Mrs Lyons *rapidly pulls out the padding from beneath her dress. Amongst it is a shawl which she uses to wrap around the baby before picking it up from the pram.*

Mrs Lyons   Thank you, Mrs Johnstone, thank you. I'll see you next week.

Mrs Johnstone   I'm due back tomorrow.

Mrs Lyons   I know, but why don't . . . why don't you take the week off, on full pay of course.

Mrs Lyons *exits.*

Mrs Johnstone *turns and enters her house with the remaining twin in the pram.*

Kid One (*off*)   What happened to the other twin, Mother?

Kid Two (*off*)   Where's the other twinny, Mam?

Mrs Johnstone   He's gone. He's gone up to heaven, love. He's living with Jesus and the angels.

Kid Three (*off*)   What's it like there, Mam, in heaven?

Mrs Johnstone   It's lovely, son, he'll be well looked after there. He'll have anything he wants.

Kid One (*off*)   Will he have his own bike?

Mrs Johnstone   Yeh. With both wheels on.

Kid One (*off*)   Why can't I have a bike? Eh?

Mrs Johnstone   I'll . . . I'll have a look in the catalogue next week. We'll see what the bikes are like in there.

Kids (*together, off*)
    Mam, I want a Meccano set.
    You said I could have a new dress, Mother.
    Why can't I have an air pistol?
    Let's look in the catalogue now, Mam.
    It's great when we look in the catalogue, Mam.
    Go on; let's all look in the catalogue.

Mrs Johnstone   I've told y', when I get home, I've got to go to work.

Mr and **Mrs Lyons** *enter their house and we see them looking at the child in its cot.*

Mrs Johnstone *enters and immediately goes about her work.*

Mrs Johnstone *stops work for a moment and glances into the cot, beaming and cooing.* **Mr Lyons** *is next to her with* **Mrs Lyons** *in the background, obviously agitated at* **Mrs Johnstone**'*s fussing.*

Mrs Johnstone   Aw, he's really comin' on now, isn't he, Mr Lyons? I'll bet y' dead proud of him, aren't y', aren't y', eh?

Mr Lyons (*good-naturedly*)   Yes . . . yes I am, aren't I, Edward? I'm proud of Jennifer, too.

Mr Lyons *beams at his wife who can hardly raise a smile.*

Mrs Johnstone   Ah . . . he's lovely. (*She coos into the cot.*) Ah look, he wants to be picked up, I'll just . . .

Mrs Lyons   No, no, Mrs Johnstone. He's fine. He doesn't want to be picked up.

Mrs Johnstone   Ah, but look, he's gonna cry . . .

Mrs Lyons   If he needs picking up, I shall pick him up. All right?

Mrs Johnstone   Well, I just thought, I'm sorry, I . . .

Mrs Lyons   Yes. Erm, has the bathroom been done? Time is getting on.

Mrs Johnstone   Oh. Yeh, yeh . . .

She exits.

Mr Lyons   Darling, don't be hard on the woman. She only wanted to hold the baby. All women like to hold babies, don't they?

Mrs Lyons   I don't want her to hold the baby, Richard. She's . . . I don't want the baby to catch anything. Babies catch things very easily, Richard.

Mr Lyons   All right, all right, you know best.

Mrs Lyons   You don't see her as much as I do. She's always fussing over him; any opportunity and she's cooing and cuddling as if she were his mother. She's always bothering him, Richard, always. Since the baby arrived she ignores most of her work. (*She is about to cry.*)

Mr Lyons   Come on, come on . . . It's all right, Jennifer. You're just a little . . . It's this depression thing that happens after a woman's had a . . .

Mrs Lyons   I'm not depressed, Richard; it's just that she makes me feel . . . Richard, I think she should go.

Mr Lyons   And what will you do for help in the house?

Mrs Lyons   I'll find somebody else. I'll find somebody who doesn't spend all day fussing over the baby.

Mr Lyons (*glancing at his watch*)   Oh well, I suppose you know best. The house is your domain. Look, Jen, I've got a board meeting. I really must dash.

Mrs Lyons   Richard, can you let me have some cash?

Mr Lyons   Of course.

Mrs Lyons   I need about fifty pounds.

Mr Lyons   My God, what for?

Mrs Lyons   I've got lots of things to buy for the baby, I've got the nursery to sort out . . .

Mr Lyons   All right, all right, here. (*He hands her the money.*)

He exits.

Mrs Lyons *considers what she is about to do, and then calls.*

Mrs Lyons   Mrs Johnstone. Mrs Johnstone, would you come out here for a moment, please.

Mrs Johnstone *enters.*

Mrs Johnstone   Yes?

Mrs Lyons   Sit down. Richard and I have been talking it over and, well, the thing is, we both think it would be better if you left.

Mrs Johnstone   Left where?

Mrs Lyons   It's your work. Your work has deteriorated.

Mrs Johnstone   But I work the way I've always worked.

Mrs Lyons   Well, I'm sorry, we're not satisfied.

Mrs Johnstone   What will I do? How are we gonna live without my job?

Mrs Lyons   Yes, well, we've thought of that. Here, here's . . . (*She pushes the money into* **Mrs Johnstone**'s *hands.*) It's a lot of money . . . but, well . . .

Mrs Johnstone (*thinking, desperate; trying to get it together*)   OK. All right. All right, Mrs Lyons, right. If I'm goin', I'm takin' my son with me, I'm takin' . . .

As **Mrs Johnstone** *moves towards the cot* **Mrs Lyons** *roughly drags her out of the way.*

Mrs Lyons   Oh no, you're not. Edward is my son. Mine.

Mrs Johnstone   I'll tell someone . . . I'll tell the police . . . I'll bring the police in an' . . .

Mrs Lyons   No . . . no, you won't. You gave your baby away. Don't you realise what a crime that is? You'll be locked up. You sold your baby.

Mrs Johnstone, *horrified, sees the bundle of notes in her hand, and throws it across the room.*

Mrs Johnstone   I didn't . . . You told me, you said I could see him every day. Well, I'll tell someone, I'm gonna tell . . .

Mrs Johnstone *starts to leave but* **Mrs Lyons** *stops her.*

Mrs Lyons   No. You'll tell nobody.

Music.

Because . . . because if you tell anyone . . . and these children learn of the truth, then you know what will happen, don't you? You do know what they say about twins, secretly parted, don't you?

Mrs Johnstone (*terrified*)   What? What?

Mrs Lyons   They . . . they say that if either twin learns that he once was a pair, they shall both immediately die. It means, Mrs Johnstone, that these brothers shall grow up unaware of the other's existence. They shall be raised apart and never, ever told what was once the truth. You won't tell anyone about this, Mrs Johnstone, because if you do, you will kill them.

Mrs Lyons *picks up the money and thrusts it into* **Mrs Johnstone***'s hands.* **Mrs Lyons** *turns and walks away. The* **Narrator** *enters.*

Narrator (*singing*)
Shoes upon the table
An' a spider's been killed.
Someone broke the lookin' glass.
A full moon shinin'
An' the salt's been spilled.
You're walkin' on the pavement cracks
Don't know what's gonna come to pass.

Now y' know the devil's got your number,
Y' know he's gonna find y',
Y' know he's right behind y',
He's starin' through your windows
He's creepin' down the hall.

Ain't no point in clutching
At your rosary
You're always gonna know what was done
Even when you shut your eyes you still see
That you sold a son
And you can't tell anyone.

But y' know the devil's got your number,
Y' know he's gonna find y',
Y' know he's right behind y',

He's starin' through your windows
He's creeping down the hall.

Yes, y' know the devil's got your number
He's gonna find y'
Y' know he's right behind y',
He's standin' on your step
And he's knocking at your door.
He's knocking at your door,
He's knocking at your door.

The **Narrator** *exits.*

During the song **Mrs Johnstone** *has gone to her house and locked herself in.*

Mickey *aged seven is knocking incessantly at the door. He is carrying a toy gun.*

Mrs Johnstone (*screaming, off*)   Go away!

Mickey   Mother . . . will y' open the bleedin' door or what?

Mrs Johnstone (*realising; with relief, off*)   Mickey?

Mrs Johnstone *comes to open the door.*

Mickey   Mam, Mam.

She grabs him and hugs him. He extricates himself.

Why was the door bolted? Did you think it was the rent man?

She laughs and looks at him.

Mam, our Sammy's robbed me other gun an' that was me best one. Why does he rob all me things off me?

Mrs Johnstone   Because you're the youngest, Mickey. It used to happen to our Sammy when he was the youngest.

Mickey   Mam, we're playin' mounted police an' Indians. I'm a Mountie. Mam, Mam, y' know this mornin', we've wiped out three thousand Indians.

Mrs Johnstone   Good.

Mickey (*aiming the gun at her and firing*)   Mam, Mam, you're dead.

Mrs Johnstone (*staring at him*)   Hmm.

Mickey   What's up, Mam?

Mrs Johnstone   Nothin', son. Go on, you go out an' play, there's a good lad. But, 'ey, don't you go playin' with those hooligans down at the rough end.

Mickey (*on his way out*)   We're down at the other end, near the big houses in the park.

Mrs Johnstone   Mickey! Come here.

Mickey   What?

Mrs Johnstone   What did you say, where have you been playin'?

Mickey   Mam, I'm sorry, I forgot.

Mrs Johnstone   What have I told you about playin' up near there? Come here. (*She grabs him.*)

Mickey   It wasn't my fault. Honest.

Mrs Johnstone   So whose fault was it then?

Mickey   The Indians. They rode up that way, they were tryin' to escape.

Mrs Johnstone   Don't you ever go up there. Do you hear me?

Mickey   Yeh. You let our Sammy go up there.

Mrs Johnstone   Our Sammy's older than you.

Mickey   But why –

Mrs Johnstone   Just shut up. Never mind why. You don't go up near there. Now go on, get out an' play. But you stay outside the front door where I can see y'.

Mickey   Ah but, Mam, the –

Mrs Johnstone   Go on!

She exits.

Mickey *makes his way outside. He is fed up. Desultory. Shoots down a few imaginary Indians but somehow the magic has gone out of genocide.*

He sits, bored, looking at the ants on the pavement.

Mickey (*reciting*)
I wish I was our Sammy
Our Sammy's nearly ten.
He's got two worms and a catapult
An' he's built a underground den.
But I'm not allowed to go in there,
I have to stay near the gate,
Cos me mam says I'm only seven,
But I'm not, I'm nearly eight!

I sometimes hate our Sammy,
He robbed me toy car y' know,
Now the wheels are missin' an' the top's broke off,
An' the bleedin' thing won't go.
An' he said when he took it, it was just like that,
But it wasn't, it went dead straight,
But y' can't say nott'n when they think y' seven
An' y' not, y' nearly eight.

I wish I was our Sammy,
Y' wanna see him spit,
Straight in y' eye from twenty yards
An' every time a hit.
He's allowed to play with matches,
And he goes to bed dead late,
And I have to go at seven,
Even though I'm nearly eight.

Y' know our Sammy,
He draws nudey women,
Without arms, or legs, or even heads
In the baths, when he goes swimmin'.
But I'm not allowed to go to the baths,

Me mam says I have to wait,
Cos I might get drowned, cos I'm only seven,
But I'm not, I'm nearly eight.

Y' know our Sammy,
Y' know what he sometimes does?
He wees straight through the letter box
Of the house next door to us.
I tried to do it one night,
But I had to stand on a crate,
Cos I couldn't reach the letter box
But I will by the time I'm eight.

Bored and petulant, **Mickey** *sits and shoots an imaginary* **Sammy**.

Edward, *also aged seven, appears. He is bright and forthcoming.*

Edward   Hello.

Mickey (*suspiciously*)   Hello.

Edward   I've seen you before.

Mickey   Where?

Edward   You were playing with some other boys near my house.

Mickey   Do you live up in the park?

Edward   Yes. Are you going to come and play up there again?

Mickey   No. I would do but I'm not allowed.

Edward   Why?

Mickey   Cos me mam says.

Edward   Well, my mummy doesn't allow me to play down here actually.

Mickey   Gis a sweet.

Edward   All right. (*He offers a bag from his pocket.*)

Mickey (*shocked*)   What?

Edward   Here.

Mickey (*trying to work out the catch; suspiciously taking one*)   Can I have another one. For our Sammy?

Edward   Yes, of course. Take as many as you want.

Mickey (*taking a handful*)   Are you soft?

Edward   I don't think so.

Mickey   Round here if y' ask for a sweet, y' have to ask about, about twenty million times. An' y' know what?

Edward (*sitting beside* **Mickey**)   What?

Mickey   They still don't bleedin' give y' one. Sometimes our Sammy does but y' have to be dead careful if our Sammy gives y' a sweet.

Edward   Why?

Mickey   Cos, if our Sammy gives y' a sweet he's usually weed on it first.

Edward (*exploding in giggles*)   Oh, that sounds like super fun.

Mickey   It is. If y' our Sammy.

Edward   Do you want to come and play?

Mickey   I might do. But I'm not playin' now cos I'm pissed off.

Edward (*awed*)   Pissed off. You say smashing things, don't you? Do you know any more words like that?

Mickey   Yeh. Yeh, I know loads of words like that. Y' know, like the 'F' word.

Edward (*clueless*)   Pardon?

Mickey   The 'F' word.

Edward *is still pulled.* **Mickey** *looks round to check that he cannot be overheard, then whispers the word to* **Edward**. *The two of them immediately wriggle and giggle with glee.*

Edward   What does it mean?

Mickey   I don't know. It sounds good though, doesn't it?

Edward   Fantastic. When I get home I'll look it up in the dictionary.

Mickey   In the what?

Edward   The dictionary. Don't you know what a dictionary is?

Mickey   Course I do . . . It's a, it's a thingy, innit?

Edward   A book which explains the meaning of words.

Mickey   The meaning of words, yeh. Our Sammy'll be here soon. I hope he's in a good mood. He's dead mean sometimes.

Edward   Why?

Mickey   It's cos he's got a plate in his head.

Edward   A plate. In his head?

Mickey   Yeh. When he was little, me mam was at work an' our Donna Marie was supposed to be lookin' after him but he fell out the window an' broke his head. So they took him to the hospital an' put a plate in his head.

Edward   A plate. A dinner plate?

Mickey   I don't think so, cos our Sammy's head's not really that big. I think it must have been one of them little plates that you have bread off.

Edward   A side plate?

Mickey   No, it's on the top.

Edward   And . . . and can you see the shape of it, in his head?

Mickey   I suppose, I suppose if y' looked under his hair.

Edward (*after a reflective pause*)   You know the most smashing things. Will you be my best friend?

Mickey   Yeh. If y' want.

Edward   What's your name?

Mickey   Michael Johnstone. But everyone calls me Mickey. What's yours?

Edward   Edward Lyons.

Mickey   D' they call y' Eddie?

Edward   No.

Mickey   Well, I will.

Edward   Will you?

Mickey   Yeh. How old are y', Eddie?

Edward   Seven.

Mickey   I'm older than you. I'm nearly eight.

Edward   Well, I'm nearly eight, really.

Mickey   What's your birthday?

Edward   July the eighteenth.

Mickey   So is mine.

Edward   Is it really?

Mickey   'Ey, we were born on the same day . . . that means we can be blood brothers. Do you wanna be my blood brother, Eddie?

Edward   Yes, please.

Mickey (*producing a penknife*)   It hurts y' know. (*He puts a nick in his hand.*) Now, give us yours.

He nicks **Edward***'s hand, then they clamp hands together.*

Mickey   See, this means that we're blood brothers, an' that we always have to stand by each other. Now you say after me: 'I will always defend my brother.'

Edward   I will always defend my brother . . .

Mickey   And stand by him.

Edward   And stand by him.

Mickey   An' share all my sweets with him.

Edward   And share . . .

Sammy *leaps in front of them, gun in hand, pointed at them.*

Mickey   Hi-ya, Sammy.

Sammy   Give us a sweet.

Mickey   Haven't got any.

Edward   Yes, you have . . .

Mickey *frantically shakes his head, trying to shut* **Edward** *up.*

Edward   Yeh, I gave you one for Sammy, remember?

Sammy *laughs at* **Edward**'*s voice and* **Mickey**'*s misfortune.*

Sammy   Y' little robbin' get.

Mickey   No, I'm not. (*He hands over a sweet.*) An' anyway, you pinched my best gun.

Mickey *tries to snatch the gun from* **Sammy** *but* **Sammy** *is too fast.*

Sammy   It's last anyway. It only fires caps. I'm gonna get a real gun soon, I'm gonna get an airgun.

He goes into a fantasy shoot-out. He doesn't notice **Edward**, *who has approached him and is craning to get a close look at his head.*

Sammy (*eventually noticing*)   What are you lookin' at?

Edward   Pardon?

Mickey   That's Eddie. He lives up by the park.

Sammy   He's a friggin' poshy.

Mickey   No, he's not. He's my best friend.

Sammy (*snorting, deciding it's not worth the bother*)   You're soft. Y' just soft little kids. (*In quiet disdain he moves away.*)

Mickey   Where y' goin'?

Sammy (*looking at* **Mickey**)   I'm gonna do another burial. Me worms have died again.

Mickey (*excitedly, to* **Edward**)   Oh, y' comin' the funeral? Our Sammy is having a funeral. Can we come, Sammy?

Sammy *puts his hand into his pocket and brings forth a handful of soil.*

Sammy   Look, they was alive an' wrigglin' this mornin'. But by dinner time they was dead.

Mickey *and* **Edward** *inspect the deceased worms in* **Sammy***'s hand.*

Mrs Johnstone *enters.*

Mrs Johnstone   Mickey . . . Mickey . . .

Edward   Is that your mummy?

Mickey   Ma . . . Mam, this is my brother.

Mrs Johnstone (*stunned*)   What?

Mickey   My blood brother, Eddie.

Mrs Johnstone   Eddie, Eddie who?

Edward   Edward Lyons, Mrs Johnstone.

Mrs Johnstone *stands still, staring at him.*

Mickey   Eddie's my best friend, Mam. He lives up by the park an' –

Mrs Johnstone   Mickey . . . get in the house.

Mickey   What?

Mrs Johnstone   Sammy, you an' all. Both of y' get in.

Sammy   But I'm older than him, I don't have to –

Mrs Johnstone   I said get, the pair of y'.

Mickey (*going, almost in tears*)   But I haven't done nothin'. I'll see y', Eddie. Ta ra, Eddie . . .

Mickey *exits.*

Mrs Johnstone   Sammy!

Sammy   Ah. (*To* **Edward**.) I'll get you.

Edward   Have I done something wrong, Mrs Johnstone?

Mrs Johnstone   Does your mother know that you're down here?

Edward *shakes his head.*

Mrs Johnstone   An' what would she say if she did know?

Edward   I . . . I think she'd be angry?

Mrs Johnstone   So don't you think you better get home before she finds out?

Edward   Yes.

Mrs Johnstone   Go on, then.

Edward *turns to go, then stops.*

Edward   Could I . . . would it be all right if I came to play with Mickey on another day? Or perhaps he could come to play at my house . . .

Mrs Johnstone   Don't you ever come round here again. Ever.

Edward   But . . .

Mrs Johnstone   Ever! Now go on. Beat it, go home before the bogey man gets y'.

Edward *walks towards his home. As he goes* **Mrs Johnstone** *sings.*

Mrs Johnstone
> Should we meet again,
> I will not recognise your name,
> You can be sure
> What's gone before
> Will be concealed.

Your friends will never learn
That once we were
On easy terms.

Mr *and* **Mrs Lyons** *enter their house as* **Edward** *walks home.*

Edward *reaches his home and walks in. His mother hugs him and his father produces a toy gun for him.* **Edward**, *delighted, seizes it and 'shoots' his father, who spiritedly 'dies' to* **Edward**'s *great amusement.* **Edward** *and his father romp on the floor.* **Mrs Lyons** *settles herself in an armchair with a storybook, calling* **Edward** *over to her.*
Edward *goes and sits with her,* **Mr Lyons** *joining them and sitting on the arm of the chair.*

Mrs Johnstone *turns and goes into her house at the end of the song.*

Mr Lyons *gets up and walks towards the door.*

Edward   Daddy . . . we haven't finished the story yet.

Mr Lyons   Mummy will read the story, Edward. I've got to go to work for an hour.

Mrs Lyons *gets up and goes to her husband,* **Edward** *goes to the bookshelf and leafs through a dictionary.*

Mrs Lyons   Richard, you didn't say . . .

Mr Lyons   Darling, I'm sorry, but if, if we complete this merger I will, I promise you, have more time. That's why we're doing it, Jen. If we complete this, the firm will run itself and I'll have plenty of time to spend with you both.

Mrs Lyons   I just – it's not me, it's Edward. You should spend more time with him. I don't want – I don't want him growing away from you.

Edward   Daddy, how do you spell bogey man?

Mr Lyons   Ask Mummy. Darling, I'll see you later now. Must dash.

He exits.

Edward   Mummy, how do you spell bogey man?

Mrs Lyons   Mm?

Edward   Bogey man?

Mrs Lyons (*laughing*)   Edward, wherever did you hear such a thing?

Edward   I'm trying to look it up.

Mrs Lyons   There's no such thing as a bogey man. It's a – a superstition. The sort of thing a silly mother might say to her children – 'The bogey man will get you.'

Edward   Will he get me?

Mrs Lyons   Edward, I've told you, there's no such thing.

A doorbell is heard.

Mrs Lyons *goes to answer the door.*

Mickey (*off*)   Does Eddie live here?

Mrs Lyons (*off*)   Pardon?

Mickey (*off*)   Does he? Is he comin' out to play, eh?

Edward (*shouting*)   Mickey!

Mickey *enters, pursued by* **Mrs Lyons**.

Mickey   Hi-ya, Eddie. I've got our Sammy's catapult. Y' comin' out?

Edward   Oh! (*He takes the catapult and tries a practice shot.*) Isn't Mickey fantastic, Mum?

Mrs Lyons   Do you go to the same school as Edward?

Mickey   No.

Edward   Mickey says smashing things. We're blood brothers, aren't we, Mickey?

Mickey   Yeh. We were born on the same day.

Edward   Come on, Mickey, let's go . . .

Mrs Lyons   Edward . . . Edward, it's time for bed.

Edward   Mummy. It's not.

Mrs Lyons *takes over and ushers* **Mickey** *out.*

Mrs Lyons   I'm very sorry, but it's Edward's bedtime.

Edward   Mummy. Mummy, it's early.

Mrs Lyons *exits with* **Mickey** *to show him out, then she returns.*

Edward   Mummy!

Mrs Lyons   Edward. Edward, where did you meet that boy?

Edward   At his house.

Mrs Lyons   And . . . and his second name is Johnstone, isn't it?

Edward   Yes. And I think you're very, very mean.

Mrs Lyons   I've told you never to go where that boy – where boys like that live.

Edward   But why?

Mrs Lyons   Because, because you're not the same as him. You're not, do you understand?

Edward   No, I don't understand. And I hate you!

Mrs Lyons *(almost crying)*   Edward, Edward, don't. It's . . . what I'm doing is only for your own good. It's only because I love you, Edward.

Edward   You don't, you don't. If you loved me you'd let me go out with Mickey because he's my best friend. I like him more than you.

Mrs Lyons   Edward. Edward, don't say that. Don't ever say that.

Edward   Well. Well, it's true. And I will say it. I know what you are.

Mrs Lyons   What? What!

Edward   You're . . . you're a fuckoff!

Mrs Lyons *hits* **Edward** *hard and instinctively.*

Mrs Lyons   You see, you see why I don't want you mixing with boys like that! You learn filth from them and behave like this – like a, like a horrible little boy, like them. But you are not like them. You are my son, mine, and you won't, you won't ever . . .

She notices the terror in **Edward**'*s face and realises how heavy she has been. Gently she pulls him to her and cradles him.*

Mrs Lyons   Oh, my son . . . my beautiful, beautiful son.

The scene fades as the next scene begins. We hear cap guns and the sound of children making Indian whoops.

The children rush on into the street playing cowboys and Indians; cops and robbers; goodies and baddies, etc.

During the battle **Mrs Lyons** *exits.*

Edward *remains onstage, in the background, as though in his garden, watching, unnoticed by the battling children.*

Mickey *and* **Linda** *are in one gang,* **Sammy** *in another.*

Sammy (*singing a cappella, kids' rhyme*)
    I got y'
    I shot y'
    An' y bloody know I did
    I got y'
    I shot y'

Linda   I stopped it with the bin lid.

There is a mass of derisive jeers from the other side. Music.

    (*Singing.*) But you know that if you cross your fingers
    And if you count from one to ten
    You can get up off the ground again
    It doesn't matter
    The whole thing's just a game.

The shooting starts all over again. A **Kid** *raps on the door of a house.* **Linda***, as a 'Moll' appears.*

Kid

> My name is Eliot Ness,
> And, lady, here's my card,
> I'm lookin' for one Al Capone

(*To* **Lackeys**.)

> Mac, check the back
> Sarge, you check the yard!

Linda

> But, pal, I've told y'
> Al ain't home.

We see 'Al' make a break for it. 'Ness' shoots him like he was eating his breakfast.

Kid   So, lady, can I use your telephone?

As Ness goes to the phone and orders a hearse we see Al get up and sing the chorus with the other children.

All

> But you know that if you cross your fingers,
> And if you count from one to ten,
> You can get up off the ground again,
> It doesn't matter
> The whole thing's just a game.

The **Kid** *who was playing Al becomes a cowboy. He turns to face* **Sammy** *and sings.*

Kid

> When I say draw,
> You'd better grab that gun,
> An' maybe say a little prayer
> Cos I'm the fastest draw
> That man you ever saw.
> Call up your woman, say goodbye to her,
> Cos y' know you're goin' right down there.

As he draws his gun on **Sammy**, **Sammy** *produces a bazooka and blows him off the stage.*

All
> But you know that if you cross your fingers,
> And if you count from one to ten,
> You can get up off the ground again,
> It doesn't matter
> The whole thing's just a game.

A small group of children become a brigade of US troops.

Sergeant
> OK, men, let's get them
> With a hand grenade.

Corporal   Let's see them try and get outta this.

Rest
> He's a hotshot Sergeant
> From the Ninth Brigade
> He's never been known to miss.

Sergeant (*to grenade*)   C'mon, give Daddy a kiss. (*He pulls the pin and lobs it.*)

His brigade cover their ears and crouch down. **Linda** *catches the grenade and lobs it back at them. After being blown to pieces they get up singing the chorus, along with the 'enemy'.*

All
> But you know that if you cross your fingers,
> And if you count from one to ten.
> You can get up off the ground again,
> It doesn't matter,
> The whole thing's just a game.

Sammy *comes forward as 'Professor Howe' carrying a condom filled with water.*

Sammy
> My name's Professor Howe,
> An' zees bomb I 'old,
> Eet can destroy ze 'emisphere,
> I've primed it, I've timed it

To explode,
Unless you let me out of here (NO?)

They don't.

Then I suggest you cover your ears.

There is an explosion which tops them all. Out of it come all the children singing the chorus.

All
But you know that if you cross your fingers,
And if you count from one to ten,
You can get up off the ground again,
It doesn't matter,
The whole thing's just a game
The whole thing's just a game
The whole thing's just a . . .

Sammy (*interrupting; chanting*)
You're dead
Y' know y' are
I got y' standin'
Near that car.

Linda
But when y' did
His hand was hid
Behind his back
His fingers crossed
An' so he's not.

Mickey   So you fuck off!

All the children, apart from **Mickey** *and* **Linda**, *point and chant the accusing 'Aah!'* **Mickey** *is singled out, accused. The rest, led by* **Sammy**, *suddenly chant at* **Mickey** *and point.*

All (*chanting*)
You said the 'F' word
You're gonna die
You'll go to hell an' there you'll fry

Just like a fish in a chip shop fat
Only twenty-five million times hotter than that!

They all laugh at **Mickey**.

Linda *moves in to protect* **Mickey** *who is visibly shaken.*

Linda   Well, well, all youse lot swear, so you'll all go to hell
with him.

Sammy   No, we won't, Linda.

Linda   Why?

Sammy   Cos when we swear . . . we cross our fingers!

Mickey   Well, my fingers were crossed.

Children (*variously*)   No they weren't. / Liar! / Come off it. /
I seen them.

Linda   Leave him alone!

Sammy   Why? What'll you do about it if we don't?

Linda (*undaunted; approaching* **Sammy**)   I'll tell my mother
why all her ciggies always disappear when you're in our house.

Sammy   What?

Linda   An' the half-crowns.

Sammy (*suddenly*)   Come on, gang, let's go. We don't wanna
play with these anyway. They're just kids.

The other children fire a barrage of 'shots' at **Mickey** *and* **Linda**
before they rush off.

Linda   I hate them!

She notices **Mickey** *quietly crying.*

Linda   What's up?

Mickey   I don't wanna die.

Linda   But y' have to, Mickey. Everyone does. (*She starts to dry
his tears.*) Like your twinny died, didn't he, when he was a baby.

See, look on the bright side of it, Mickey. When you die you'll meet your twinny again, won't y'?

Mickey   Yeh.

Linda   An' listen, Mickey, if y' dead, there's no school, is there?

Mickey (*smiling*)   An' I don't care about our Sammy, anyway. Look. (*He produces an air pistol.*) He thinks no one knows he's got it. But I know where he hides it.

Linda (*impressed*)   Ooh . . . gis a go.

Mickey   No . . . Come on, let's go get Eddie first.

Linda   Who?

Mickey   Come on, I'll show y'.

They go as if to **Edward***'s garden.*

Mickey (*loud but conspiratorially*)   Eddie . . . Eddie . . . comin' out?

Edward   I . . . My mum says I haven't got to play with you.

Mickey   Well, my mum says I haven't got to play with you. But take no notice of mothers. They're soft. Come on, I've got Linda with me. She's a girl but she's all right.

Edward *decides to risk it and creeps out.*

Mickey   Hi-ya.

Edward   Hi-ya, Mickey. Hello, Linda.

Linda   Hi-ya, Eddie. (*She produces the air pistol.*) Look . . . we've got Sammy's airgun.

Mickey   Come on, Eddie. You can have a shot at our target in the park.

Linda   Peter Pan.

Mickey   We always shoot at that, don't we, Linda?

Linda   Yeh, we try an' shoot his little thingy off, don't we, Mickey?

They all laugh.

Come on, gang, let's go.

Edward (*standing firm*)   But Mickey . . . I mean . . . suppose we get . . . caught . . . by a policeman.

Mickey   Aah . . . take no notice. We've been caught loads of times by a policeman . . . haven't we, Linda?

Linda   Oh, my God, yeh. Hundreds of times. More than that.

Mickey   We say dead funny things to them, don't we, Linda?

Edward   What sort of funny things?

Linda   All sorts, don't we, Mickey?

Mickey   Yeh . . . like, y' know, when they ask what y' name is, we say things like, like 'Adolf Hitler', don't we, Linda?

Linda   Yeh, an' hey, Eddie, y' know when they say, 'What d' y' think you're doin'?' we always say somethin' like, like, 'Waitin' for the ninety-two bus.'

Mickey and **Linda** *crease up with laughter.*

Linda   Come on.

Edward (*greatly impressed*)   Do you . . . do you really? Goodness, that's fantastic.

Mickey   Come on, bunk under y' fence, y' ma won't see y'.

Mickey, **Linda** and **Edward** *exit.*

Mrs Lyons *enters the garden.*

Mrs Lyons (*calling*)   Edward, Edward, Edward . . .

The **Narrator** *enters*

Music.

Narrator (*singing*)
   There's gypsies in the wood,
   An' they've been watchin' you,
   They're gonna take your baby away.
   There's gypsies in the wood,
   An' they've been calling you,
   Can Edward please come out and play,
   Please can he come with us and play.

   You know the devil's got your number,
   Y' know he's gonna find y',
   Y' know he's right behind y',
   He's staring through your windows,
   He's creeping down the hall.

Mr Lyons *enters the garden.*

Mrs Lyons   Oh Richard, Richard.

Mr Lyons   For God's sake, Jennifer, I told you on the phone, he'll just be out playing somewhere.

Mrs Lyons   But where?

Mr Lyons   Outside somewhere, with friends. Edward . . .

Mrs Lyons   But I don't want him out playing.

Mr Lyons   Jennifer, he's not a baby.

Mrs Lyons   I don't care, I don't care . . .

Mr Lyons   For Christ's sake, you bring me home from work in the middle of the day, just to say you haven't seen him for an hour. Perhaps we should be talking about you getting something for your nerves.

Mrs Lyons   There's nothing wrong with my nerves. It's just . . . just this place . . . I hate it. Richard, I don't want to stay here any more. I want to move.

Mr Lyons   Jennifer! Jennifer, how many times . . . the factory is here, my work is here . . .

Mrs Lyons   It doesn't have to be somewhere far away. But we have got to move, Richard. Because if we stay here I feel that something terrible will happen, something bad.

Mr Lyons *sighs and puts his arm round* **Mrs Lyons**.

Mr Lyons   Look, Jen. What is this thing you keep talking about getting away from? Mm?

Mrs Lyons   It's just . . . it's these people . . . these people that Edward has started mixing with. Can't you see how he's drawn to them? They're . . . drawing him away from me.

Mr Lyons, *in despair, turns away from her.*

Mr Lyons   Oh Christ.

He turns to look at her but she looks away. He sighs and absently bends to pick up a pair of children's shoes from the floor.

I really do think you should see a doctor.

Mrs Lyons (*snapping*)   I don't need to see a doctor. I just need to move away from this neighbourhood, because I'm frightened. I'm frightened for Edward.

Mr Lyons *places the shoes on the table before turning on her.*

Mr Lyons   Frightened of what, woman?

Mrs Lyons (*wheeling to face him*)   Frightened of . . . (*She is stopped by the sight of the shoes on the table. She rushes at the table and sweeps the shoes off.*)

Narrator (*singing*)
   There's shoes upon the table
   An' a spider's been killed
   Someone broke the lookin' glass
   There's a full moon shinin'
   An' the salt's been spilled
   You're walkin' on pavement cracks
   Don't know what's gonna come to pass.

   Now you know the devil's got your number
   He's gonna find y'

Y' know he's right behind y'
He's starin' through your windows
He's creeping down the hall.

The song ends with a percussion build to a sudden full stop and the scene snaps from **Mrs Lyons** *to the children.*

Mickey, Eddie *and* **Linda** *are standing in line, taking it in turns to fire the air pistol.* **Mickey** *takes aim and fires.*

Linda (*with glee*)   Missed.

Edward *loads and fires.*

Linda   Missed!

Linda *takes the gun and fires. We hear a metallic ping. She beams a satisfied smile at* **Mickey** *who ignores it and reloads, fires. The routine is repeated with exactly the same outcome until:*

Mickey (*taking the gun*)   We're not playin' with the gun no more. (*He puts it away.*)

Linda   Ah, why?

Mickey   It gets broke if y' use it too much.

Edward   What are we going to do now, Mickey?

Mickey   I dunno.

Linda   I do.

Mickey   What?

Linda   Let's throw some stones through them windows.

Mickey (*brightening*)   Ooh, I dare y', Linda, I dare y'.

Linda (*bending for a stone*)   Well, I will. I'm not scared, either. Are you, Eddie?

Edward   Erm . . . well . . . erm . . .

Linda   He is, look. Eddie's scared.

Mickey   No, he isn't! Are y', Eddie?

Edward (*stoically*)   No . . . I'm not. I'm not scared at all, actually.

Linda   Right, when I count to three we all throw together. One, two, three . . .

Unseen by them a **Policeman** *has approached behind them.*

Policeman   Me mother caught a flea, she put it in the tea pot to make a cup of tea . . . And what do you think you're doing?

Linda *and* **Mickey** *shoot terrified glances at* **Edward**, *almost wetting themselves.*

Edward (*mistaking their look for encouragement*)   Waiting for the ninety-two bus. (*He explodes with excited laughter.*)

Linda   He's not with us.

Mickey   Sir.

Linda   Sir.

Policeman   No. He's definitely with us. What's your name, son?

Edward   Adolf Hitler.

Edward *laughs until through the laughter he senses that all is not well. He sees that he alone is laughing. The laughter turns to tears which sets the other two off.*

The three children turn round, crying, bawling, followed by the **Policeman**.

The three children exit. **Mrs Johnstone** *enters.*

The **Policeman** *goes to confront* **Mrs Johnstone**.

Policeman   And he was about to commit a serious crime, love. Now, do you understand that? You don't wanna end up in court again, do y'?

Mrs Johnstone *shakes her head.*

Policeman   Well, that's what's gonna happen if I have any more trouble from one of yours. I warned you last time, didn't I, Mrs Johnstone, about your Sammy?

Mrs Johnstone *nods.*

Policeman   Well, there'll be no more bloody warnings from now on. Either you keep them in order, missis, or it'll be the courts for you, or worse, won't it?

Mrs Johnstone *nods.*

Policeman   Yes, it will.

As the **Policeman** *turns and goes towards the* **Lyons** *house music is heard.*

Mrs Johnstone (*singing*)
    Maybe some day
    We'll move away
    And start all over again
    In some new place
    Where they don't know my face
    And nobody's heard of my name
    Where we can begin again
    Feel we can win an' then . . .
    Maybe . . .

The music tails off as we see the **Policeman** *confronting* **Mr Lyons**. *The* **Policeman** *has removed his helmet and holds a glass of Scotch.* **Edward** *is there.*

Policeman   An', er, as I say, it was more of a prank, really, Mr Lyons. I'd just dock his pocket money if I was you. (*Laughs.*) But, one thing I would say, if y' don't mind me sayin', is, well, I'm not sure I'd let him mix with the likes of them in the future. Make sure he keeps with his own kind, Mr Lyons. Well, er, thanks for the drink, sir. All the best now. He's a good lad, aren't you, Adolf? Goodnight, sir. (*He replaces his helmet.*)

The **Policeman** *leaves.*

Mr Lyons   Edward . . . how would you like to move to another house?

Edward   Why, Daddy?

Mr Lyons   Erm, well, various reasons really. Erm, actually Mummy's not been too well lately and we thought a move, perhaps further out towards the country somewhere, might . . . Do you think you'd like that?

Edward   I want to stay here.

Mr Lyons   Well, you think about it, old chap.

Edward *leaves his home and goes to the* **Johnstones***' door. He knocks at the door.*

Mrs Johnstone *answers the door.*

Edward   Hello, Mrs Johnstone. How are you?

Mrs Johnstone   You what?

Edward   I'm sorry. Is there something wrong?

Mrs Johnstone   No, I just . . . I don't usually have kids enquiring about my health. I'm . . . I'm all right. An' how are you, Master Lyons?

Edward   Very well, thank you.

Mrs Johnstone *looks at* **Edward** *for a moment.*

Mrs Johnstone   Yeh. You look it. Y' look very well. Does your mother look after you?

Edward   Of course.

Mrs Johnstone   Now listen, Eddie, I told you not to come around here again.

Edward   I'm sorry, but I just wanted to see Mickey.

Mrs Johnstone   No. It's best . . . if . . .

Edward   I won't be coming here again. Ever. We're moving away. To the country.

Mrs Johnstone   Lucky you.

Edward   But I'd much rather live here.

Mrs Johnstone   Would you? When are y' goin'?

Edward   Tomorrow.

Mrs Johnstone   Oh. So we really won't see you again, eh . . .

Edward *shakes his head and begins to cry.*

Mrs Johnstone   What's up?

Edward (*through his tears*)   I don't want to go. I want to stay here where my friends are . . . where Mickey is.

Mrs Johnstone   Come here.

She takes him. Cradles him, letting him cry.

No, listen . . . listen, don't you be soft. You'll probably love it in your new house. You'll meet lots of new friends an' in no time at all you'll forget Mickey ever existed.

Edward   I won't . . . I won't. I'll never forget.

Mrs Johnstone   Shush, shush. Listen, listen, Eddie, here's you wantin' to stay here, an' here's me, I've been tryin' to get out for years. We're a right pair, aren't we, you an' me?

Edward   Why don't you, Mrs Johnstone? Why don't you buy a new house near us?

Mrs Johnstone   Just like that?

Edward   Yes, yes.

Mrs Johnstone   'Ey.

Edward   Yes.

Mrs Johnstone   Would you like a picture of Mickey, to take with you? So's you could remember him?

Edward   Yes, please.

She removes a locket from around her neck.

Mrs Johnstone   See, look . . . there's Mickey, there. He was just a young kid when that was taken.

Edward   And is that you, Mrs Johnstone?

She nods.

Can I really have this?

Mrs Johnstone   Yeh. But keep it a secret, eh, Eddie? Just our secret, between you an' me.

Edward (*smiling*)   All right, Mrs Johnstone. (*He puts the locket round his neck*)

He looks at her a moment too long.

Mrs Johnstone   What y' lookin' at?

Edward   I thought you didn't like me. I thought you weren't very nice. But I think you're smashing.

Mrs Johnstone (*looking at him*)   God help the girls when you start dancing.

Edward   Pardon?

Mrs Johnstone   Nothing. (*Calling into the house.*) Mickey, say goodbye to Eddie – he's moving.

Mickey *comes out of the house. Music is quietly introduced.*

Edward *moves to* **Mickey** *and gives him a small parcel from his pocket.* **Mickey** *unwraps a toy gun. The two boys clasp hands and wave goodbye.* **Mrs Johnstone** *and* **Mickey** *watch as* **Edward** *joins his parents, dressed in outdoor clothes, on their side of the stage.*

Edward   Goodbye.

Mr Lyons   Well, Edward . . . do you like it here?

Edward (*unenthusiastically*)   It's very nice.

Mrs Lyons   Oh, look, Edward . . . look at those trees and those cows. Oh Edward, you're going to like it so much out here, aren't you?

Edward   Yes. Are you feeling better now, Mummy?

Mrs Lyons   Much better now, darling. Oh Edward, look, look at those birds . . . Look at that lovely black-and-white one . . .

Edward (*immediately covering his eyes*)   Don't Mummy, don't look. It's a magpie, never look at one magpie. It's one for sorrow . . .

Mr Lyons   Edward . . . that's just stupid superstition.

Edward   It's not, Mickey told me.

Mrs Lyons   Edward, I think we can forget the silly things that Mickey said.

Edward   I'm going inside. I want to read.

He exits.

Mr Lyons (*comforting his wife*)   Children take time to adapt to new surroundings. He'll be as right as rain in a few days. He won't even remember he once lived somewhere else.

Mrs Lyons *forces a smile and allows herself to be led inside by her husband.*

Mickey *rings the doorbell of* **Edward**'s *old house. A* **Woman** *answers the door.*

Woman   Yes?

Mickey   Is er . . . is Eddie in?

Woman   Eddie? I'm afraid Eddie doesn't live here now.

Mickey   Oh, yeh. (*He stands looking at the* **Woman**.)

Woman   Goodbye.

Mickey   Do y' . . . erm, do y' know where he lives now?

Woman   Pardon?

Mickey   See, I've got some money, I was gonna go, on the bus, an' see him. Where does he live now?

Woman   I'm afraid I've no idea.

Mickey   It's somewhere in the country, isn't it?

Woman   Look, I honestly don't know and I'm rather busy. Goodbye.

The **Woman** *closes the door on* **Mickey**.

Mickey *wanders away, aimless and bored, deserted and alone.*

Music.

Mickey (*singing*)
    No kids out on the street today,
    You could be living on the moon.
    Maybe everybody's packed their bags and moved away,
    Gonna be a long, long, long,
    Sunday afternoon.

    Just killing time and kicking cans around,
    Try to remember jokes I knew,
    I tell them to myself, but they're not funny since I found
    It's gonna be a long, long, long,
    Sunday afternoon.

Edward *in his garden, equally bored and alone. The scene appears in such a way that we don't know if it is real or in* **Mickey***'s mind.*

Mickey
    My best friend
    Always had sweets to share, (he)
    Knew every word in the dictionary.
    He was clean, neat and tidy,
    From Monday to Friday,
    I wish that I could be like,
    Wear clean clothes, talk properly like,
    Do sums and history like −

Edward *and* **Mickey** (*together*)
    My friend.

Edward
    My best friend
    He could swear like a soldier
    You would laugh till you died
    At the stories he told y'
    He was untidy
    From Monday to Friday
    I wish that I could be like

Kick a ball and climb a tree like
Run around with dirty knees like

Edward *and* **Mickey** (*together*)
My friend.

The lights fade on **Edward** *as the music shifts back to 'Long Sunday Afternoon'.*

Mickey
Feels like everybody stayed in bed
Or maybe I woke up too soon.
Am I the last survivor
Is everybody dead?
On this long, long, long,
Sunday afternoon.

Mrs Johnstone *appears, clutching a letter.*

Mrs Johnstone (*singing*)
Oh, bright new day,
We're movin' away.

Mickey (*speaking*)   Mam? What's up?

Mrs Johnstone (*singing*)
We're startin' all over again.

Donna Marie *enters together with various* **Neighbours**.

Donna Marie (*speaking*)   Is it a summons, Mother?

Mrs Johnstone (*singing*)
Oh, bright new day,
We're goin' away.

Mickey (*calling*)   Sammy!

Mrs Johnstone *addresses the various onlookers.*

Mrs Johnstone (*singing*)
Where nobody's heard of our name.

Sammy *enters.*

Sammy (*speaking*)   I've never robbed nothin', honest, Mam.

Mrs Johnstone (*singing*)
>   Where we can begin again.
>   Feel we can win and then
>   Live just like livin' should be
>   Got a new situation,
>   A new destination,
>   And no reputation following me.

Mickey (*speaking*)   What is it, what is it?

Mrs Johnstone (*singing*)
>   We're goin' out,
>   We're movin' house
>   We're starting all over again.
>   We're leavin' this mess
>   For our new address (*pointing it out*)
>   'Sixty-five Skelmersdale Lane'.

Mickey (*speaking, worried*)   Where's that, Mam?

Sammy (*speaking*)   Is that in the country?

Donna Marie (*speaking*)   What's it like there?

Mrs Johnstone (*singing*)
>   The air is so pure,
>   You get drunk just by breathing,
>   And the washing stays clean on the line.
>   Where there's space for the kids,
>   Cos the garden's so big,
>   It would take you a week just to reach the far side.

(*Speaking*) Come on, Sammy, Mickey, now you've all gorra help. (*To the* **Neighbours**, *in a 'posh' voice.*) Erm, would you excuse us, we've gorra pack. We're movin' away.

Mrs Johnstone *and the children go in to pack.*

Neighbour   What did she say?

Milkman   They're movin' away.

All   Praise the Lord, He has delivered us at last.

Neighbour
    They're gettin' out,
    They're movin' house,
    Life won't be the same as in the past.

Policeman
    I can safely predict
    A sharp drop in the crime rate.

Neighbour
    It'll be calm an' peaceful around here.

Milkman
    AND now I might even
    Get paid what is mine, mate.

Neighbour   An' you'll see, graffiti will soon disappear.

Mrs Johnstone *marches out of the house carrying battered suitcases, followed by the children who are struggling to get out some of the items mentioned in the verse.*

Mrs Johnstone
    Just pack up the bags,
    We're leavin' the rags,
    The wobbly wardrobe, chest of drawers that never close.
    The two-legged chair, the carpet so bare,
    You wouldn't see it if it wasn't for the holes.
    Now that we're movin'
    Now that we're improvin',
    Let's just wash our hands of this lot.
    For it's no longer fitting, for me to be sitting
    On a sofa I know for a fact was knocked off.

Her last line is delivered to **Sammy** *who indicates the* **Policeman**, *trying to get her to shut up.*

Mrs Johnstone
    We might get a car,
    Be all 'lardie dah',
    An' go drivin' out to the sands.
    At the weekend
    A gentleman friend,

Might take me dancing
To the local bands.
We'll have a front room,
And then if it should happen,
That His Holiness flies in from Rome,
He can sit there with me, eating toast, drinking tea
In the sort of surroundings that remind him of home.

Mickey (*speaking*)   It's like the country, isn't it, Mam?

Mrs Johnstone (*speaking*)   'Ey, we'll be all right out here, son, away from the muck an' the dirt an' the bloody trouble. Eh, I could dance. Come here.

Mickey   Get off . . .

Mrs Johnstone *picks up a picture of the Pope which is lying next to one of the suitcases and begins to dance.*

Mrs Johnstone (*singing*)
Oh, bright new day,
We're movin' away,
We're startin' all over again.
Oh, bright new day,
We're goin' away,
Where nobody's heard of our name.

(*Speaking.*) An' what are you laughin' at?

Mickey   I'm not laughin', I'm smilin'. I haven't seen you happy like this for ages.

Mrs Johnstone   Well, I am happy now. Eh, Jesus, where's the others?

Mickey   They went into that field, Mam.

Mrs Johnstone   Sammy. Sammy! Get off that bleedin' cow before I kill you. Oh Jesus, what's our Donna Marie stepped into? Sammy, that cow's a bull. Come here the pair of you.

Now we can begin again,
Feel we can win an' then
Live just like livin' should be.

Got a new situation,
A new destination,
An' no reputation following me.

All

We're gettin' out. We're movin' house
We're goin' away. Gettin' out today.
We're movin' movin' movin' house.

Mrs Johnstone

We're goin' away,
Oh, bright new day.

Curtain.

Act Two

Mrs Johnstone *moves forward to sing.*

Mrs Johnstone
　　The house we got was lovely,
　　The neighbours are a treat,
　　They sometimes fight on Saturday night,
　　But never in the week.

Mrs Johnstone *turns and looks 'next door'. Raised voices, and a dog barking, are heard, off.*

Neighbours (*off, speaking*)　What time do you call this then? Time I got shot of you, ratbag!

Dog *barks.*

Mrs Johnstone (*singing*)
　　Since I pay me bills on time, the milkman
　　Insists I call him Joe. He brings me bread and eggs.

Joe, *the milkman, enters.*

Mrs Johnstone
　　Says I've got legs
　　Like Marilyn Monroe.

Mrs Johnstone *and* **Joe** *dance.*

Mrs Johnstone
　　Sometimes he takes me dancing
　　Even takes me dancing.

Joe *exits, dancing.*

Mrs Johnstone
　　I know our Sammy burnt the school down
　　But it's very easily done.
　　If the teacher lets the silly gets
　　Play with magnesium.
　　Thank God he only got probation.

A **Judge** *is seen, ticking* **Sammy** *off.*

Mrs Johnstone
The Judge was old and slow.

She sings to the **Judge**, *laying on a smile for him.*

Mrs Johnstone
Though it was kind of him,
Said I reminded him of Marilyn Monroe.

Judge (*slightly scandalised*)
And could I take you dancing?
Take you dancing.

Mrs Johnstone *takes the* **Judge**'s *gavel and bangs him on the head.*

The **Judge** *exits, stunned.*

Mrs Johnstone
Our Mickey's just turned fourteen
Y'know he's at *that* age.

Mickey *is seen in his room.*

Mrs Johnstone
When you mention girls, or courting,
He flies into a rage.

Mickey (*speaking*)   Shut up talking about me, Mother.

Mrs Johnstone
He's got a thing for taking blackheads out,
And he thinks that I don't know,
That he dreams all night of girls who look like
Marilyn Monroe.
He's even started dancing, secret dancing,

(*Slower*) And as for the rest, they've flown the nest
Got married or moved away
Our Donna Marie's already got three, she's
A bit like me that way . . .

(*Slower*) And that other child of mine,
 I haven't seen for years, although

Each day I pray he'll be OK,
Not like Marilyn Monroe . . .

On the other side of the stage **Mrs Lyons** *enters, waltzing with a very awkward fourteen-year-old* **Edward**.

Mrs Lyons (*speaking*)   One, two, three. One, two three.

(*Singing.*) Yes, that's right, you're dancing.
That's right, you're dancing.

(*Speaking.*) You see, Edward, it is easy.

Edward   It is if you have someone to practise with. Girls. But in term time we hardly ever see a girl, let alone dance with one.

Mrs Lyons   I'll give you some more lessons when you're home for half-term. Now come on, come on, you're going to be late. Daddy's at the door with the car. Now, are you sure you've got all your bags?

Edward   Yes, they're in the boot.

Mrs Lyons (*looking at him*)   I'll see you at half-term then, darling. (*She kisses him, a light kiss, but holds on to him.*) Look after yourself, my love.

Edward   Oh Mummy . . . stop fussing . . . I'm going to be late.

Mrs Lyons   We have had a very good time this holiday, though, haven't we?

Edward   We always do.

Mrs Lyons   Yes. We're safe here, aren't we?

Edward   Mummy, what are you on about? Sometimes . . .

A car horn is heard.

Mrs Lyons (*hustling him out, good-naturedly*)   Go on, go on . . . There's Daddy getting impatient. Bye, bye, Edward.

Edward   Bye, Ma.

He exits.

We see **Mrs Johnstone** *hustling* **Mickey** *to school.*

Mrs Johnstone You're gonna be late, y' know. Y' late already.

Mickey I'm not.

Mrs Johnstone You're gonna miss the bus.

Mickey I won't.

Mrs Johnstone Well, you'll miss Linda, she'll be waitin' for y'.

Mickey Well, I don't wanna see her. What do I wanna see her for?

Mrs Johnstone (*laughing at his transparency*) You've only been talkin' about her in your sleep for the past week . . .

Mickey (*outraged*) You liar . . .

Mrs Johnstone 'Oh, my sweet darling . . . '

Mickey I never. That was – a line out the school play!

Mrs Johnstone (*her laughter turning to a smile*) All right. I believe y'. Now go before you miss the bus. Are y' goin'?

We see **Linda** *at the bus stop.*

Linda Hi-ya, Mickey.

Mrs Johnstone Ogh, did I forget? Is that what you're waitin' for? Y' waitin' for y' mum to give y' a big sloppy kiss, come here . . .

Mickey I'm goin', I'm goin' . . .

Sammy *runs through the house, pulling on a jacket as he does so.*

Sammy Wait for me, YOU.

Mrs Johnstone Where you goin', Sammy?

Sammy (*on his way out*) The dole.

Mickey *and* **Sammy** *exit.*

Mrs Johnstone *stands watching them as they approach the bus stop. She smiles at* **Mickey**'*s failure to cope with* **Linda**'*s smile of welcome.*

The 'bus' appears, with the **Narrator** *as the conductor.*

Conductor   Come on, if y' gettin' on. We've not got all day.

Sammy, **Mickey** *and* **Linda** *get on the 'bus'.*

Mrs Johnstone (*calling to her kids*)   Tarrah, lads. Be good, both of y' now. I'll cook a nice surprise for y' tea.

Conductor (*noticing her as he goes to ring the bell*)   Gettin' on, missis?

Mrs Johnstone *shakes her head, still smiling.*

Conductor (*speaking*)
Happy are y'? Content at last?
Wiped out what happened, forgotten the past?

She looks at him, pulled.

But you've got to have an endin', if a start's been made.
No one gets off without the price bein' paid.

The 'bus' pulls away as the **Conductor** *begins to collect fares.*

No one can embark without the price bein' paid.

(*To* **Mickey**.) Yeh?

Mickey (*handing over his money*)   A fourpenny scholar.

Conductor   How old are y'?

Linda   He's fourteen. Both of us are. A fourpenny scholar for me as well.

The **Conductor** *gives out the ticket as* **Sammy** *offers his money.*

Sammy   Same for me.

Conductor   No, son.

Sammy   What?

Conductor   You're older than fourteen.

Mickey (*worried*)   Sammy . . .

Sammy   Shut it. (*To the* **Conductor**.) I'm fourteen. I wanna fourpenny scholar.

Conductor   Do you know the penalty for tryin' to defraud –

Sammy   I'm not defraudin' no one.

Conductor (*shouting to the driver*)   'Ey, Billy, take the next left, will y'? We've got one for the cop shop here.

Sammy   What? (*He stands.*)

Mickey   He didn't mean it, mister. Don't be soft. He, he was jokin'. Sammy, tell him, tell him you're really sixteen. I'll lend you the rest of the fare . . .

Sammy (*considers, then*)   Fuck off. (*He produces a knife. To the* **Conductor**.) Now move, you. Move! Give me the bag.

Music.

Mickey   Sammy . . . Sammy . . .

Sammy (*to the* **Conductor**)   I said give. Stop the bus.

The **Conductor** *rings the bell to stop the 'bus'.*

Sammy   Come on, Mickey.

Linda   You stay where y' are, Mickey. You've done nothin'.

Mickey   Sammy, Sammy, put that away . . . it's still not too late. (*To the* **Conductor**.) Is it, mister?

Sammy   Mickey.

Linda   He's stayin' here.

Sammy   No-mark!

Sammy *leaps from the 'bus' and is pursued by two policemen. The 'bus' pulls away leaving* **Mickey** *and* **Linda** *alone on the pavement.*

Linda   He'll get put away for this, y' know, Mickey.

Mickey   I know.

Linda   He's always been a soft get, your Sammy.

Mickey   I know.

Linda   You better hadn't do anything soft, like him.

Mickey   I wouldn't.

Linda   Y' better hadn't or I won't be in love with y' any more!

Mickey   Shut up! Y' always sayin' that.

Linda   I'm not.

Mickey   Yis y' are. Y' bloody well said it in assembly yesterday.

Linda   Well, I was only tellin' y'.

Mickey   Yeh, an' five hundred others as well.

Linda   I don't care who knows. I just love you. I love you!

Mickey   Come on . . . we're half an hour late as it is.

He hurries off, followed by **Linda**.

Edward's *school where* **Edward** *is confronted by a teacher (the* **Narrator***) looking down his nose at* **Edward**.

Teacher   You're doing very well here, aren't you, Lyons?

Edward   Yes, sir. I believe so.

Teacher   Talk of Oxbridge.

Edward   Yes, sir.

Teacher   Getting rather big for your boots, aren't you?

Edward   No, sir.

Teacher   No, sir? Yes, sir. I think you're a tyke, Lyons. The boys in your dorm say you wear a locket around your neck. Is that so?

Pause.

Edward   Yes, sir.

Teacher   A locket? A locket. This is a boys' school, Lyons.

Edward   I am a boy, sir.

Teacher   They you must behave like one. Now give this locket to me.

Edward   No, sir.

Teacher   No sir? Am I to punish you, Lyons? Am I to have you flogged?

Edward   You can do exactly as you choose, sir. You can take a flying fuck at a rolling doughnut! But you shall not take my locket!

Teacher (*thunderstruck*)   I'm going to . . . I'm going to have you suspended, Lyons.

Edward   Yes, sir.

He exits.

As **Edward** *exits, a class in a secondary modern school is formed – all boredom and futility. The school bell rings. The teacher becomes the teacher of this class in which we see* **Linda** *and* **Mickey**.

Teacher   And so, we know then, don't we, that the Boro Indian of the Amazon Basin lives on a diet of . . .

Perkins   Sir, sir . . .

Teacher   A diet of . . .

Perkins   Sir, sir . . .

Teacher   A diet of what, Johnstone? The Boro Indian of the Amazon Basin lives on a diet of what?

Mickey   What?

Teacher   Exactly, lad, exactly. What?

Mickey   I don't know.

Teacher (*his patience gone*)   Y' don't know. (*Mimicking.*) You don't know. I told y' two minutes ago, lad.

Linda   Leave him alone, will y'?

Teacher   You just stay out of this, miss. It's got nothing to do with you. It's Johnstone, not you . . .

Perkins Sir!

Teacher Oh, shut up, Perkins, y' borin' little turd. But you don't listen, do you, Johnstone?

Mickey (*shrugging*) Yeh.

Teacher Oh, y' do? Right, come out here in front of the class. Now then, what is the staple diet of the Boro Indian of the Amazon Basin?

Mickey *looks about for help. There is none.*

Mickey (*defiantly*) Fish fingers!

Teacher Just how the hell do you hope to get a job when you never listen to anythin'?

Mickey It's borin'.

Teacher Yes, yes, you might think it's boring but you won't be sayin' that when you can't get a job.

Mickey Yeh. Yeh, an' it'll really help me to get job if I know what some soddin' pygmies in Africa have for their dinner!

The class erupts into laughter.

Teacher (*to class*) Shut up. Shut up.

Mickey Or maybe y' were thinkin' I was lookin' for a job in an African restaurant.

Teacher Out!

Linda Take no notice, Mickey. I love you.

Teacher Johnstone, get out!

Linda Oh, leave him alone, you. Y' big worm!

Teacher Right, you as well . . . out . . . out . . .

Linda I'm goin' . . . I'm goin' . . .

Teacher You're both suspended.

Linda *and* **Mickey** *leave the class.*

The classroom sequence breaks up as we see **Mrs Lyons** *staring at a piece of paper.* **Edward** *is standing before her.*

Mrs Lyons (*incredulously*)   Suspended? Suspended? (*She looks at the paper.*) Because of a locket?

Edward   Because I wouldn't let them have my locket.

Mrs Lyons   But what's so . . . Can I see this locket?

There is a pause.

Edward   I suppose so . . . If you want to.

He takes off the locket from around his neck and hands it to his mother. She looks at it without opening it.

Mrs Lyons   Where did you get this?

Edward   I can't tell you that. It's a secret.

Mrs Lyons (*finally smiling in relief*)   I know, it's from a girlfriend, isn't it? (*She laughs.*) Is there a picture in here?

Edward   Yes, Mummy. Can I have it back now?

Mrs Lyons   You won't let Mummy see your girlfriend. Oh, Edward, don't be so . . . (*She playfully moves away.*) Is she beautiful?

Edward   Mummy, can . . .

Mrs Lyons   Oh, let me look, let me look. (*She beams a smile at him and then opens the locket.*)

Music.

Edward   Mummy . . . Mummy, what's wrong . . . ? (*He goes to her and holds her steady.*) Mummy!

Mrs Lyons *takes his arms away from her.*

Edward   What is it?

Mrs Lyons   When . . . when were you photographed with this woman?

Edward   Pardon?

Mrs Lyons   When? Tell me, Edward.

Edward *begins to laugh.*

Mrs Lyons   Edward!

Edward   Mummy . . . you silly old thing. That's not me.
That's Mickey.

Mrs Lyons   What?

Edward   Mickey . . . you remember, my friend when I was
little. (*He takes the locket and shows it to her.*) Look. That's Mickey . . .
and his mother. Why did you think it was me? (*He looks at it.*)
I never looked a bit like Mickey.

He replaces the locket around his neck.

Mrs Lyons *watches him.*

Mrs Lyons   No, it's just . . . (*She stares, deep in thought.*)

Edward (*looking at her*)   Are you feeling all right, Mummy?
You're not ill again, like you used to be . . . are you?

Mrs Lyons   Where did you get that . . . locket from, Edward?
Why do you wear it?

Edward   I can't tell you that, Ma. I've explained, it's a
secret, I can't tell you.

Mrs Lyons   But . . . but I'm your mother.

Edward   I know, but I still can't tell you. It's not important,
I'm going up to my room. It's just a secret, everybody has
secrets, don't you have secrets?

He exits to his room.

The **Narrator** *enters.*

Music continues.

Narrator (*singing*)
    Did you really feel that you'd become secure
    That time had brushed away the past
    That there's no one by the window, no one knocking on
        your door

Did you believe that you were free at last
Free from the broken looking glass.

Oh y' know the devil's got your number
He's never far behind you
He always knows where to find you
And someone said they'd seen him walking past your door.

The **Narrator** *exits.*

We see **Mickey** *and* **Linda** *making their way up the hill,* **Linda**
having some difficulty in high-heeled shoes.

Linda   Tch . . . you didn't tell me it was gonna be over a load
of fields.

Mickey   I didn't tell y' nothin'. I didn't ask y' to come, y'
followed me. (*He walks away from her.*)

Linda (*watching him walk away*)   Mickey, Mickey . . . I'm stuck
. . . (*Holding out her helpless arms.*) Me foot's stuck. Honest.

Mickey *goes back, timidly takes a wrist and ineffectually pulls.*

Linda   Mickey, I think y' might be more successful if you
were to sort of put your arms around here. (*She puts her hands on
her waist.*) Oh Mickey, be gentle, be gentle . . .

Mickey (*managing to pull her free*)   Will you stop takin' the piss
out of me!

Linda   I'm not, I'm not.

Mickey *points down in the direction they have come from.*

Mickey   Look . . . y' can see the estate from up here.

Linda   Have we come all this way just to look at the bleedin'
estate? Mickey, we're fourteen.

She beams at him. He can't take it and looks the other way.

Mickey   Look.

Linda   What?

Mickey   There's that lad lookin' out the window. I see him sometimes when I'm up here.

Linda   Oh . . . he's gorgeous, isn't he?

Mickey   What?

Linda   He's lovely lookin', isn't he?

Mickey   All right, all right! You've told me once.

Linda   Well, he is. An' what do you care if I think another feller's gorgeous, eh?

Mickey   I don't.

Linda   You . . . I give up with you, Mickey Johnstone. I'm off. You get on my bleedin' nerves.

Linda *exits.*

Mickey   What . . . Linda . . . Linda . . . Don't . . . Linda, I wanna kiss y', an' put me arms around y' an' kiss y' and kiss y' an even fornicate with y' but I don't know how to tell y', because I've got pimples an' me feet are too big an' me bum sticks out an' . . .

He becomes conscious of **Edward** *approaching, and affects nonchalance.*

Mickey (*speaking*)
If I was like him
I'd know (*singing*) all the right words

Edward
If I was like . . . him
I'd know some real birds
Apart from those in my dreams
And in magazines.

Mickey
Just look at his hair

Edward
His hair's dark and wavy
Mine's mousey to fair

Mickey
Mine's the colour of gravy

Edward *and* **Mickey** (*together*)
Each part of his face
Is in just the right place

Edward
He's laughing at me
At my nose, did he notice

Mickey
I should wear a brace

Edward
That I've got halitosis

Edward *and* **Mickey** (*together*)
When nature picked on me
She chose to stick on me

Edward
Eyes that don't match

Mickey
And ears that stand out

Edward *and* **Mickey** (*together*)
She picked the wrong batch
When she handed mine out
And then she attacked me
With permanent acne

Edward
I wish I was a bit like
Wish that I could score a hit like
And be just a little bit like
That guy
That guy

Mickey
I wish that I could be like
Just a little less like me
Like the sort of guy I see, like

That guy
That guy.

Edward   Hi.

Mickey   Hi. Gis a ciggie?

Edward   Oh, I don't smoke actually. But I can go and get you some.

Mickey   Are you soft? (*He suddenly realises.*) A blood brother.

Edward   Mickey? Well, shag the vicar.

Mickey *laughs.*

Edward   What's wrong?

Mickey   You, it sounds dead funny swearin' in that posh voice.

Edward   What posh voice?

Mickey   That one.

Edward   Well, where do you live?

Mickey   The estate, look. (*He points.*)

Edward   My God, I only live . . .

Mickey   I know.

Edward   That girl I saw you with, was that . . .

Mickey   Linda. Do you remember Linda?

Edward   Wow, was that Linda? And is she your girlfriend?

Mickey   Yeh. She's one of them.

Edward   One of them.

Mickey   Have you got a girlfriend?

Edward   Me? Me? No!

Mickey   Haven't y'?

Edward   Look, you seem to have rather a lot of them, erm . . . perhaps you'd share one with me.

Mickey   Share one? Eddie, I haven't even got one girlfriend.

Edward   But Linda . . . you said . . .

Mickey   I know, but she's not. I mean, I mean she would be me girlfriend, she even says she loves me all over the place, but it's just like dead difficult.

Edward   What?

Mickey   Like knowing what to say.

Edward   But you must, you must . . .

Mickey   I know that. But every time I see her I promise meself I'll ask her but, but the words just disappear.

Edward   But you mustn't let them.

Mickey   What do I say, though?

Edward   Mickey, it's easy, I've read about it. Look, the next time you see Linda, you stare straight into her eyes and you say, 'Linda, I love you, I want you, the very core of my being is longing for you, my loins are burning for you. Let me lay my weary head between your warm breasts!' And then, Mickey, her eyes will be half closed and her voice may appear somewhat husky as she pleads with you, 'Be gentle with me, be gentle.' It would work, you know. Listen, we can see how it's done; look, the Essoldo for one week only, *Nymphomaniac Nights* and *Swedish Au Pairs.* Whoa . . .

Mickey   I'll have to go home and get some money . . .

As the boys are going, we see **Mrs Lyons** *appear. She has seen* **Edward** *and* **Mickey** *and she stares after them. Making up her mind she quickly goes and fetches a coat, then follows the two boys.*

The **Narrator** *enters.*

Music.

Edward   I've got plenty, I'll lend –

Mickey   No, it's all right, me mam'll give it me . . .

Edward   Come on then, before my ma sees me. She's off her beam, my ma . . .

The boys exit, followed by **Mrs Lyons**.

Narrator (*singing*)
> Did you really feel that you'd become secure,
> And that the past was tightly locked away,
> Did you really feel that you would never be found,
> Did you forget you've got some debts to pay,
> Did you forget about the reckoning day?
>
> Yes, the devil he's still got your number,
> He's moved in down the street from you,
> Someone said he wants to speak to you,
> Someone said they'd seen him leanin' on your door.

The **Narrator** *exits.*

We see **Mrs Johnstone** *in her kitchen as* **Mickey** *bursts in followed by* **Edward**.

Mickey   Mother, Mam, look, look it's Eddie . . . Eddie . . .

Mrs Johnstone *stands looking at* **Edward** *and smiling.*

Edward   Hi-ya, Mrs Johnstone. Isn't it fantastic? We're neighbours again.

Mickey   Mum, Mum, Mum, Eddie lives in that house, y' know, that big house on the hill. Mam, can y' lend us a quid to go to the pictures?

Mrs Johnstone   Yes, it's, erm . . . it's in the sideboard . . .

Mickey   Oh thanks, Mam. I love y'.

He exits to the next room.

Edward   You're looking very well, Mrs Johnstone.

Mrs Johnstone   Am I? Do you . . . do you still keep that locket I gave y'?

Edward   Of course . . . Look . . .

Mickey *enters.*

Mickey   Mam, Mam, can I bring Eddie back afterwards, for coffee?

Mrs Johnstone   Yeh. Go on . . . go an' enjoy yourselves, but don't be too late, will y'?

Mickey   See y', Mam.

Edward   Bye, Mrs Johnstone.

The boys prepare to leave.

Mrs Johnstone   'Ey. What's the film you're gonna see?

Edward   Erm, what?

Mrs Johnstone   What film . . .

Edward *and* **Mickey** (*together*)   *Dr Zhivago.* / *Magnificent Seven.*

Mrs Johnstone   *Dr Zhivago's Magnificent Seven.*

Edward   It's a double bill.

Mrs Johnstone   I see. An' where's it on?

Edward *and* **Mickey** (*together*)   What? / The Essoldo.

Mrs Johnstone   Oh . . . the Essoldo, eh? When I passed the Essoldo this mornin' they were showin' *Nymphomaniac Nights* and *Swedish Au Pairs.*

Edward   Ah yes, Mrs Johnstone, yes, yeh, they're just the trailers: a documentary and . . .

Mickey   An' a travelogue. About Sweden!

Mrs Johnstone   Do the pair of you really think I was born yesterday?

Edward *can't hold it any longer and breaks into embarrassed laughter.*

Mickey (*trying to hold on*)   It is, it . . . it's just a travelogue . . .

Mrs Johnstone   Showing the spectacular bends and curves of Sweden . . . Go on, y' randy little sods.

Mickey (*scandalised*)   Mother!

Mrs Johnstone   Go on before I throw a bucket of water over the pair of y' . . .

Mickey *drags* **Edward** *out.*

Mrs Johnstone   I don't know about coffee . . . you'd be better off with bromide. (*She gets on with her work.*)

Edward (*outside the house but looking back*)   . . . She's fabulous your ma, isn't she?

Mickey   She's a fuckin' headcase. Come on.

As they run off we see **Mrs Lyons** *appear from where she has been concealed in the alley.*

Mrs Johnstone *is lilting the 'We Go Dancing' line as* **Mrs Lyons** *appears in the kitchen.* **Mrs Johnstone** *gets a shock as she looks up and sees* **Mrs Lyons** *there. The two women stare at each other.*

Mrs Johnstone (*eventually nodding*)   Hello.

Mrs Lyons   How long have you lived here?

Pause.

Mrs Johnstone   A few years.

Pause.

Mrs Lyons   Are you always going to follow me?

Mrs Johnstone   We were rehoused here . . . I didn't follow –

Mrs Lyons   Don't lie! I know what you're doing to me! You gave him that locket, didn't you? Mm?

Mrs Johnstone *nods.*

Mrs Lyons   He never takes it off, you know. You're very clever, aren't you?

Mrs Johnstone   I . . . I thought I'd never see him again. I wanted him to have a picture of me . . . even though he'd never know.

Mrs Lyons   Afraid he might eventually have forgotten you? Oh no. There's no chance of that. He'll always remember you.

After we'd moved he talked less and less of you and your family. I started . . . just for a while I came to believe that he was actually mine.

Mrs Johnstone   He is yours.

Mrs Lyons   No. I took him. But I never made him mine. Does he know? Have you told –

Mrs Johnstone   Of course not!

Mrs Lyons   Even when – when he was a tiny baby I'd see him looking straight at me and I'd think, he knows . . . he knows. (*Pause.*) You have ruined me. (*Pause.*) But you won't ruin Edward! Is it money you want?

Mrs Johnstone   What?

Mrs Lyons   I'll get it for you. If you move away from here. How much?

Mrs Johnstone   Look . . .

Mrs Lyons   How much?

Mrs Johnstone   Nothin'! Nothing. (*Pause.*) You bought me off once before . . .

Mrs Lyons   Thousands . . . I'm talking about thousands if you want it. And think what you could do with money like that.

Mrs Johnstone   I'd spend it. I'd buy more junk and trash; that's all. I don't want your money. I've made a life out here. It's not much of one maybe, but I made it. I'm stayin' here. You move if you want to.

Mrs Lyons   I would. But there's no point. You'd just follow me again, wouldn't you?

Mrs Johnstone   Look, I'm not followin' anybody.

Mrs Lyons   Wherever I go you'll be just behind me. I know that now . . . always and for ever and ever like, like a shadow unless I can . . . make . . . you go . . . But you won't, so . . .

We see that throughout the above **Mrs Lyons** *has opened the knife drawer and has a lethal-looking kitchen knife in her hand.* **Mrs Johnstone**, *unaware, has her back to her. On impulse, and punctuated by a note,* **Mrs Johnstone** *wheels. On a punctuated note* **Mrs Lyons** *lunges again but* **Mrs Johnstone** *manages to get hold of her wrist, rendering the knife hand helpless.* **Mrs Johnstone** *takes the knife from* **Mrs Lyons**'*s grasp and moves away.*

Mrs Johnstone (*staring at her; knowing*)   YOU'RE MAD. MAD.

Mrs Lyons (*quietly*)   I curse the day I met you. You ruined me.

Mrs Johnstone   Go. Just go!

Mrs Lyons   Witch. (*Suddenly pointing.*) I curse you. Witch!

Mrs Johnstone (*screaming*)   Go!

Mrs Lyons *exits to the street.*

Kids' *voices are heard, chanting, off.*

Kids (*off*)
High upon the hill the mad woman lives,
Never ever eat the sweets she gives,
Just throw them away and tell your dad,
High upon a hill there's a woman gone mad.

Mad woman, mad woman living on the hill,
If she catches your eye then you never will
Grow any further, your teeth will go bad
High upon a hill there's a woman gone mad.

Edward *and* **Mickey** *emerge from the cinema, blinking as they try to adjust to the glare of the light in the street. They are both quite overcome with their celluloid/erotic encounter. As they pause and light up cigarettes by a corner lamp post they groan in their ecstatic agony. Each is in an aroused trance.*

Mickey   Ooh . . . !

Edward   Naked knockers, ooh . . . !

Mickey   Naked knockers with nipples . . . !

Edward   Playing tennis. Ooh. Tennis with tits. Will Wimbledon ever be the same?

Mickey   Tits!

Edward   Tits, tits, tits . . . (*He begins a frustrated chant of the word, oblivious to everything.*)

Linda *and a mate enter.*

Finally **Mickey** *realises* **Linda***'s presence and knocks* **Edward***, who becomes aware of the girls' presence. He goes into a song without missing a beat.*

Edward
    Tits, tits, tits a lovely way,
    To spend an evening . . .

He grabs **Linda***'s* **Mate** *and begins to waltz her around the street.*

Edward
    Can't think of anything I'd rather do . . .

Mate (*simultaneously with the above*)   Gerroff. Put me down, get y' friggin' paws off me, you. Linda. Y' bloody lunatic, gettoff.

Edward *finally releases her and bows.*

Mate   Linda, come on. I'm goin' . . .

The **Mate** *begins to walk away.* **Linda** *makes no attempt to follow.*

Linda   What y' doin' in town, Mick?

Mickey   We've erm, we've . . .

Edward   We have been undergoing a remarkable celluloid experience!

Mate   We'll miss the bus, Linda.

Mickey   We've been the pictures.

Linda   So have we. What did y' go see?

Edward *and* **Mickey** (*together*)   *Nympho*— / *Bridge Over the River Kwai.*

Linda   Ah, we've seen that. We went to see *Nymphomaniac Nights* instead. An' *Swedish Au Pairs*.

Mickey   You what?

Edward *begins to laugh.*

Mate   Oh, sod y' then. I'm goin'.

The **Mate** *exits.*

Mickey (*to* **Edward**)   What are you laughin' at? Take no notice. Remember Eddie? He's still a headcase. Shurrup.

Edward (*shouting*)   Tits. Tits, tits, tits, tits, tits.

Edward *leaps around and hopefully ends up sitting at the top of the lamp post.* **Linda** *and* **Mickey** *laugh at him, while* **Edward** *chants.*

A **Policeman** *enters.*

The three do not see the arrival of the **Policeman***.*

Policeman   An' what the bloody hell do you think you're doin'?

Edward   Adolf Hitler?

Policeman   Get down.

Edward *gets down from the lamp post.*

Policeman (*getting out his black book*)   Right. I want your names. What's your name?

Linda, **Mickey** and **Edward** (*together*)   Waitin' for the ninety-two bus!

Linda (*pointing upwards*)   Oh my God, look . . .

Policeman   Now listen . . .

The **Policeman** *falls for it and looks up. The three make their exit.*

The **Policeman** *realises and gives chase.*

Mickey, **Linda** and **Edward** *enter, laughing and exhausted. The* **Narrator** *enters.*

Narrator
   There's a few bob in your pocket and you've got good friends,
   And it seems that summer's never coming to an end,
   Young, free and innocent, you haven't got a care,
   Apart from decidin' on the clothes you're gonna wear.
   The street's turned into Paradise, the radio's singing dreams,
   You're innocent, immortal, you're just fifteen.

*The **Narrator** becomes the rifle-range man at the fairground.*

Linda, **Mickey** *and* **Edward** *pool their monry and hand it to the
rifle-range man. He gives the gun to* **Mickey***, who smiles, shakes his
head and points to* **Linda***. The man offers the gun to* **Edward** *but*
Linda *takes it. The boys indicate to the rifle-range man that he has had
it now* **Linda** *has the gun. They eagerly watch the target but their smiles
fade as* **Linda** *misses all three shots.* **Mickey** *and* **Edward** *tum on*
Linda *in mock anger. They are stopped by the rifle-range man throwing
them a coconut which is used as a ball for a game of piggy-in-the-middle.
When* **Linda** *is caught in the middle the game freezes.*

Narrator
   And who'd dare tell the lambs in spring,
   What fate the later seasons bring?
   Who'd tell the girl in the middle of the pair
   The price she'll pay for just being there?

Throughout the following we see **Linda**, **Mickey** *and* **Edward**
*suiting their actions to the words – coming out of the chip shop, talking,
lighting a cigarette by the lamp post.*

Narrator
   But leave them alone, let them go and play
   They care not for what's at the end of the day.
   For what is to come, for what might have been,
   Life has no ending when you're sweet sixteen
   And your friends are with you to talk away the night,
   Or until Mrs Wong switches off the chippy light.
   Then there's always the corner and the street lamp's glare
   An' another hour to spend, with your friends, with her,
   To share your last cigarette and your secret dream
   At the midnight hour, at seventeen.

Throughout the following we see **Linda**, **Mickey** *and* **Edward**, *as if at the beach,* **Linda** *taking a picture of* **Mickey** *and* **Edward**, *arms around each other, camping it for the camera but eventually giving good and open smiles.* **Mickey** *taking a picture of* **Edward** *and* **Linda**. **Edward** *down on one knee and kissing her hand.* **Edward** *taking a picture of* **Mickey** *and* **Linda**. **Mickey** *pulling a distorted face,* **Linda** *wagging a finger at him.* **Mickey** *chastened.* **Linda** *raising her eyebrows and putting one of his arms round her.* **Linda** *moving forward and taking the camera.* **Linda** *waving the* **Narrator** *to snap them. He goes.* **Linda** *showing the* **Narrator** *how to operate the camera.* **Linda**, **Mickey** *and* **Edward**, *grouped together, arms around each other as the* **Narrator** *takes the picture. They get the camera and wave their thanks to the* **Narrator**.

Narrator
    It's just another ferry boat, a trip to the beach
    But everything is possible, the world's within your reach
    An' you don't even notice broken bottles in the sand
    The oil in the water and you can't understand
    How living could be anything other than a dream
    When you're young, free and innocent and just eighteen.

Linda, **Mickey** *and* **Edward** *exit.*

Narrator
    And only if the three of them could stay like that for ever,
    And only if we could predict no changes in the weather,
    And only if we didn't live in life, as well as dreams,
    And only if we could stop and be for ever, just eighteen.

We see **Edward** *waiting by a street lamp.* **Linda** *approaches, sees him, and goes into a street walk.*

Linda   Well, hello, sweetie pie; looking for a good time? Ten to seven. *(She laughs.)* Good time . . . ten to seven . . . it was a joke . . . I mean, I know it was a lousy joke but y' could at least go into hysterics!

Edward *smiles.*

Linda   That's hysterics?

Edward   Where's Mickey?

Linda   He must be workin' overtime.

Edward   Oh.

Linda   What's wrong with you, misery?

Edward (*after a pause*)   I go away to university tomorrow.

Linda   Tomorrow! You didn't say.

Edward   I know. I think I've been pretending that if I didn't mention it the day would never come. I love it when we're together, the three of us, don't you?

Linda *nods.*

Edward   Can I write to you?

Linda   Yeh . . . yeh, if you want.

Edward   Would Mickey mind?

Linda   Why should he?

Edward   Come on . . . because you're his girlfriend.

Linda   No, I'm not.

Edward   You are, Linda.

Linda   I'm not, he hasn't asked me.

Edward (*laughing*)   You mean he still hasn't?

Linda (*laughing*)   No.

Edward   But it's ridiculous.

Linda   I know. I hope for his sake he never has to ask me to marry him. He'll be a pensioner before he gets around to it.

Edward (*after a pause*)   He's mad. If I was Mickey I would have asked you years ago.

Linda   I know you would. Cos y' soft, you are.

Edward (*singing*)
    If I could stand inside his shoes I'd say,
    How can I compare thee to a summer's day

Linda (*speaking*)   Oh go away . . .

Edward
    I'd take a page in all the papers,
    I'd announce it on the news
    If I was the guy, if I
    Was in his shoes.
    If I was him I'd bring you flowers
    And ask you to dance
    We'd while away the hours making future plans
    For rainy days in country lanes
    And trips to the sea.
    I'd just tell you that I love you
    If it was me.

    But I'm not saying a word,
    I'm not saying I care,
    Though I would like you to know,
    That I'm not saying a word,
    I'm not saying I care,
    Though I would like you to know.
    If I was him I'd have to tell you,
    What I've kept in my heart,
    That even if we had to live
    Some worlds apart
    There would not be a day
    In which I'd not think of you.
    If I was him, if I was him.
    That's what I'd do.

    But I'm not saying a word
    I'm not saying I care
    Though I would like you to know
    That I'm not saying a word,
    I'm not saying I care,
    Though I would like you to know.

But I'm not.

Linda   What?

Edward   Mickey.

Mickey *enters*

Edward   Mickey!

Mickey   Hi-ya, Ed. Lind.

Linda   Where've y' been?

Mickey   I had to do overtime. I hate that soddin' place.

Edward   Mickey. I'm going away tomorrow . . . to university.

Mickey   What? Y' didn't say.

Edward   I know . . . but the thing is, I won't be back until Christmas. Three months. Now you wouldn't want me to continue in suspense for all that time, would you?

Linda   What are you on about?

Edward   Will you talk to Linda?

Linda   Oh Eddie . . .

Edward   Go on . . . go on.

Mickey *turns and goes to her.* **Linda** *tries to keep a straight face.*

Mickey   Erm . . . well, the er, thing is . . . Linda, I've erm . . . (*Quickly.*) Linda for Christ's sake will you go out with me?

Linda (*just as quickly*)   Yeh.

Mickey   Oh . . . erm . . . Good. Well, I suppose I better . . . well . . . er . . . come here . . . (*He quickly embraces and kisses* **Linda**.)

Linda (*fighting for air*)   My God. Y' take y' time gettin' goin' but then there's no stoppin' y'.

Mickey   I know . . . come here . . .

They kiss again. **Edward** *turns and begins to leave.*

Mickey   Eddie . . . Eddie, where y' goin'? I thought we were all goin' the club. There's a dance.

Edward   No . . . I've got to, erm, I've got to pack for tomorrow.

Mickey   Are y' sure?

Edward *nods.*

Mickey   See y' at Christmas then, Eddie? Listen, I'm gonna do loads of overtime between now and then, so the Christmas party's gonna be on me . . . right?

Edward   Right. It's a deal, Mick. See you.

Linda *rushes across and kisses* **Edward** *lightly.*

Linda   Thanks, Eddie.

Mickey   Yeh, Eddie . . . thanks.

Linda *and* **Mickey**, *arms around each other, watch him go. They turn and look at each other.*

Mickey *and* **Linda** *exit.*

The lights crossfade to the **Johnstone** *house.* **Mickey** *enters and prepares to go to work.* **Mrs Johnstone** *enters with* **Mickey**'s *lunch bag. The* **Narrator** *enters.*

Narrator
It was one day in October when the sun began to fade,
And winter broke the promise that summer had just made,
It was one day in October when the rain came falling down,
And someone said the bogey man was seen around the town.

The **Narrator** *exits.*

Mrs Johnstone   Y' gonna be late, Mick. I don't want you gettin' the sack an' spendin' your days idlin' round like our Sammy. Come on.

Mickey, *instead of making an effort to go, stands looking at her.*

Mickey   Mam!

Mrs Johnstone   What?

Mickey   What!

Mrs Johnstone   Come on.

Mickey   Mam. Linda's pregnant!

A moment.

Mrs Johnstone   Do you love her?

Mickey   Yeh!

Mrs Johnstone   When's the weddin'?

Mickey   We thought, about a month . . . before Christmas anyway. Mam, could we live here for a bit?

She looks at him and nods.

Are you mad?

Mrs Johnstone   At you? Some hypocrite I'd be. No . . . I'm not mad, son. I'm just thinkin' . . . you've not had much of a life with me, have y'?

Mickey   Don't be stupid, course I have. You're great, you are, Mam. (*He gives her a quick kiss.*) Ta-ra, I'd better get a move on. They've started layin' people off in the other factory, y' know. Ta-ra, Mam. Thanks.

He exits.

Music.

Mrs Johnstone *watches him go. As 'Miss Jones' begins, she whips off her overalls and a wedding suit is underneath. She acquires a hat.*

A wedding party assembles. **Mickey** *remains in his working clothes.* **Linda** *is in white. Other guests are suitably attired. A managing director enters and sings as his secretary,* **Miss Jones**, *takes notes.*

Mr Lyons (*singing*)
  Take a letter, Miss Jones (quote)

  I regret to inform you,
  That owing to circumstances
  Quite beyond our control.
  It's a premature retirement
  For those surplus to requirement,
  I'm afraid it's a sign of the times, Miss Jones,
  An unfortunate sign of the times.

Throughout the next verse we see the wedding party wave goodbye to
Mickey, *who goes to work only to have his cards given to him when he gets there.*

Mr Lyons
Take a letter, Miss Jones,
Due to the world situation
The shrinking pound, the global slump,
And the price of oil
I'm afraid we must fire you,
We no longer require you,
It's just another
Sign of the times,
Miss Jones,
A most miserable sign of the times.

The **Guests** *at the wedding become a line of men looking for work.*
Mickey *joins them as* **Linda** *watches. They are constantly met with shaking heads and by the end of the following verse have assembled in the dole office.*

Mr Lyons
Take a letter, Miss Jones, of course we'll
Let the workforce know when
Inflation's been defeated
And recession is no more.
And for the moment we suggest
You don't become too depressed
As it's only a sign
Of the times,
Miss Jones,
A peculiar sign of the times.

Take a letter, Miss Jones:
My dear Miss Jones, we'd like to thank you
Many years of splendid service,
Et cetera blah blah blah
You've been a perfect poppet,
Yes that's right, Miss Jones, you've got it
It's just another sign
Of the times,

Miss Jones, it's
Just another sign of the times.

*He shows her the door. Crying, she approaches the dole queue but then
hesitates. The men in the queue take up the song.*

Dole-ites
Dry your eyes, Miss Jones
It's not as bad as it seems (you)
Get used to being idle
In a year or two.
Unemployment's such a pleasure
These days, we call it leisure
It's just another sign
Of the times,
Miss Jones, it's
Just another sign of the times.

Mickey *leaves the group and stands apart.* **Miss Jones** *takes his
place. Behind* **Mickey** *we can see* **Linda** *and his mother.*

Dole-ites
There's a young man on the street, Miss Jones,
He's walkin' round in circles,
He's old before his time,
But still too young to know.
Don't look at him, don't cry though
This living on the giro
Is only a sign of the times,
Miss Jones, it's
Just another sign of the times.

As they exit.

Miss Jones,
It's just another sign of the times . . .

Crowd *exits.*

Mickey *is left alone, sitting dejected. We hear Christmas bells.*

Edward *enters in a duffel coat and college scarf, unseen by* **Mickey**.
He creeps up behind **Mickey** *and puts his hands over his eyes.*

Edward   Guess who?

Mickey   Father Christmas.

Edward (*leaping out in front of him*)   Mickey . . . (*Laughing.*)
Merry Christmas.

Mickey, *unamused, looks at* **Edward** *and then looks away.*

Edward   Come on then . . . I'm back, where's the action,
the booze, the Christmas parties, the music and the birds?

No reaction.

What's wrong, Mickey?

Mickey   Nothin'. How's university?

Edward   Mickey, it's fantastic. I haven't been to so many
parties in my life. And there's just so many tremendous people,
but you'll meet them, Mick, some of them, Baz, Ronnie and
Clare and oh, lots of them. They're coming over to stay for the
New Year, for the party. Ooh it's just . . . it's great, Mickey.

Mickey   Good.

Edward   Come on, what's wrong? It's nearly Christmas, we
were going to do everything. How's Linda?

Mickey   She's OK.

Edward (*trying again to rally him*)   Well, come on then, let's go
then . . . come on.

Mickey   Come on where?

Edward   Mickey, what's wrong?

Mickey   You. You're a dick head!

Edward *is slightly unsure but laughs anyway.*

Mickey   There are no parties arranged. There is no booze
or music. Christmas? I'm sick to the teeth of Christmas an' it
isn't even here yet. See, there's very little to celebrate, Eddie.
Since you left I've been walking around all day, every day,
lookin' for a job.

Edward   What about the job you had?

Mickey   It disappeared. (*Pause.*) Y' know somethin', I bleedin' hated that job, standin' there all day never doin' nothin' but put cardboard boxes together. I used to get . . . used to get terrified that I'd have to do it for the rest of me life. But, but after three months of nothin', the same answer everywhere, nothin', nothin' down for y', I'd crawl back to that job for half the pay and double the hours. Just . . . just makin' up boxes it was. But after bein' fucked off from everywhere, it seems like it was paradise.

Pause.

Edward   Why . . . why is a job so important? If I couldn't get a job I'd just say, sod it and draw the dole, live like a bohemian, tilt my hat to the world and say 'screw you'. So you're not working. Why is it so important?

Mickey (*looking at him*)   You don't understand anythin', do ye? I don't wear a hat that I could tilt at the world.

Edward   Look . . . come on . . . I've got money, plenty of it. I'm back, let's forget about bloody jobs, let's go and get Linda and celebrate. Look, look, money, lots of it, have some . . . (*He tries to throw some notes into **Mickey**'s hands.*)

Mickey   No. I don't want your money, stuffit.

He throws the notes to the ground. **Edward** *picks them up and stands looking at* **Mickey**.

Mickey   Eddie, just do me a favour an' piss off, will ye?

Edward   I thought, I thought we always stuck together. I thought we were . . . were blood brothers.

Mickey   That was kids' stuff, Eddie. Didn't anyone tell y? (*He looks at **Edward**.*) But I suppose you still are a kid, aren't ye?

Edward   I'm exactly the same age as you, Mickey.

Mickey   Yeh. But you're still a kid. An' I wish I could be as well, Eddie, I wish I could still believe in all that blood brother stuff. But I can't, because while no one was looking I grew up.

An' you didn't, because you didn't need to; an' I don't blame y' for it, Eddie. In your shoes I'd be the same, I'd still be able to be a kid. But I'm not in your shoes, I'm in these, lookin' at you. An' you make me sick, right? That was all just kids' stuff, Eddie, an' I don't want to be reminded of it. Right? So just, just take yourself away. Go an' see your friends an' celebrate with them.

Pause.

Go on . . . beat it before I hit y'.

Edward *looks at* **Mickey** *and then slowly backs away.* **Sammy** *approaches* **Mickey** *as, on the other side, we see* **Linda** *hurrying on, passing* **Edward**, *who stops and calls.*

Edward   Linda!

Sammy   Mickey.

Edward   Linda.

Reluctantly she stops, goes back a few paces.

Hello, Linda.

Linda   Hello, Eddie.

Edward   Why haven't you called to see me?

Linda   I heard you had friends, I didn't like butting in.

Edward   You'd never be butting in and you know it. It wouldn't matter if I never saw those friends again, if I could be with you.

Linda   Eddie . . .

Sammy   Look, I'm offerin' . . . all we need is someone to keep the eye for us. Look at y', Mickey. What have y' got? Nothin', like me mam. Where y' takin' y' tart for New Year? Nowhere.

Edward   You might as well know, if I'm not going to see you again. I've always loved you, you must have known that.

Sammy   We don't *use* the shooters. They're just frighteners. Y' don' need to use them. Everyone behaves when they see a shooter. You won't even be where the action is. Just keep the eye out for us.

Edward   I'm sorry.

Sammy   Fifty quid, Mickey. Fifty quid for an hour's work. Just think where y' could take Linda if you had cash like that.

Edward   I'm sorry, Linda.

Linda   It's all right. I suppose, I suppose I always . . . loved you, in a way.

Edward   Then marry me.

Linda   Didn't Mickey tell y'? We got married two weeks before you came home and I'm expecting a baby.

Mickey   Fifty notes?

Sammy *nods.*

Mickey   All right.

Sammy   Great.

Mickey *nods.*

Sammy   Cheer up, will y'? It's New Year.

He exits.

Edward*'s* **Friends** (*variously, off*)   Where's Lyo? / Come on, Lyons, you pillock, you're suppond to be helping us with the booze. / Come on, Lyonese. / Edward, come on.

Linda   I'll see y', Eddie. Happy New Year. (*She moves away.*)

Edward *exits.*

Mickey   Linda . . . Linda.

Linda   Are you comin' in?

Mickey   Look . . . I'll be back about eight o'clock. An' listen, get dressed up. I'm takin' y' out.

Linda   What?

Mickey We're goin' dancin'. Right? Then we're goin' for a slap-up meal an' tomorrow you can go into town an' get some new clothes.

Linda Oh yeh? Where's the money comin' from?

Mickey I'm . . . doin' some work . . .

Linda What?

Mickey Look, stop arguin', will y'? I'm doin' some work and then I'm takin' you out.

Sammy (*off*) Mickey!

Linda Is that your Sammy?

Mickey Now shut up, Linda. Right, right? Just make sure you're ready at eight . . . (*He starts to leave.*)

Linda (*as he goes*) Mickey . . . Mickey . . . No!

She exits.

Mickey *moves away.*

The **Narrator** *enters.*

Sammy *enters.*

Narrator
      There's a full moon shining and a joker in the pack,
      The dealer's dealt the cards, and he won't take them back,
      There's a black cat stalking and a woman who's afraid,
      That there's no getting off without the price being paid.

We see **Mickey**, *nervously keeping lookout, as behind him, as if inside a filling station office, we see* **Sammy**, *his back to us, talking to an offstage character.*

Sammy Don't piss about with me, pal . . . I said give! (*Pause.*) Listen, it's not a toy, y' know . . . We're not playin' games. Y' don't get up again if one of these hits y' . . . What are you doin'? I said listen to me, I . . . don't you fuckka' touch that . . . Listen.

An alarm bell is heard, followed by an explosion from the gun. **Sammy**
reels backwards. He and **Mickey** *run and enter their house.*

Narrator
There's a man lies bleeding on a garage floor.

Sammy
Quick, get in the house an' bolt the fuckin' door.

Mickey *stands unable to move, tears streaming down his face.*

Narrator
And maybe, if you counted ten and kept your fingers crossed
It would all be just a game and then no one would have lost.

Mickey
You shot him, you shot him.

Sammy
I know I bloody did.

Mickey
You shot him, you shot him.

Sammy
Move, I've got to get this hid.

Linda (*off*)   Mickey . . . Mickey, is that you?

Sammy   Ooh, fuck . . . (*He quickly pulls back a mat, pulls up a
floorboard and puts the gun beneath it.*)

Linda *enters.*

Two **Policemen** *arrive at the house.*

Sammy *splits out the back.* **Mickey** *remains silently crying.* **Linda**
goes to him and puts her arms around him. As **Sammy** *is being
apprehended at the back, the other* **Policeman** *enters and gently removes*
Linda *from* **Mickey** *and leads hin out and into the police station.*

Linda   But I've ironed him a shirt.

Music.

Mickey, *placed in a prison cell, stands quietly crying.*

Mrs Johnstone *enters.*

Mrs Johnstone (*singing*)
    The jury found him guilty
    Sent him down for seven years,
    Though he acted like they gave him life,
    He couldn't stop the tears.
    And when we went to visit him,
    He didn't want to know,
    It seems like jail's sent him off the rails,
    Just like Marilyn Monroe
    His mind's gone dancing
    Can't stop dancing.

A **Doctor** *enters the cell and examines* **Mickey**.

    They showed him to a doctor,
    And after routine test,
    A prescription note the doctor wrote,
    For the chronically depressed.
    And now the tears have stopped
    He sits and counts the days to go
    And treats his ills with daily pills
    Just like Marilyn Monroe.

The **Doctor** *exits.*

    They stop his mind from dancing
    Stop it dancing.

A prison warder leads **Linda** *into the cell. He indicates a seat opposite* **Mickey**.

Linda   What are y' doin'?

Mickey   What? I'm takin' me tablet.

Linda   Listen, Mickey, I've told y'. They're just junk. You'll be home soon, Mickey, and you should come off them.

Mickey   Why? I need . . . I need to take them.

Linda   Listen, Mickey, you've –

Mickey   No! See, he says, the doctor, he said . . .

Linda   What did he say?

Mickey   He said, about me nerves. An' how I get depressed an' I need to take these cos they make me better . . .

Linda   I get depressed but I don't take those. You don't need those, Mickey.

Mickey   Leave me alone, will y'? I can't cope with this. I'm not well. The doctor said, didn't he, I'm not well . . . I can't do things . . . leave me alone . . .

*The **Warder** escorts **Linda** from the cell.*

*During the following verse **Mickey** leaves the prison and goes home.*

Mrs Johnstone (*singing*)
   With grace for good behaviour
   He got out before his time
   The family and the neighbours told him
   He was lookin' fine.
   But he's feelin' fifteen years older
   And his speech is rather slow
   And the neighbours said
   You'd think he was dead
   Like Marilyn Monroe
   No cause for dancing
   No more dancing . . .

Linda *approaches* **Mrs Johnstone**. **Linda** *is weighed down with shopping bags and is weary.*

Mrs Johnstone   Linda, where've y' been? We've gorra do somethin' about him. He's been out for months and he's still takin' those pills. Linda, he needs a job, you two need a place of your own an' –

Linda   Mam . . . Mam, that's why I'm late, I've been to see . . . We're movin' at the end of the month. We've got our own place an' I think I've got Mickey a job . . .

Mrs Johnstone   Oh, Jesus, thank God. But how –

Linda   It's all right . . . I . . . someone I know . . .

Mrs Johnstone   But . . .

Linda   It's all right, Mam. Did y' get our Sarah from school?

Mrs Johnstone   Yeh, she's in bed, but listen, how did y' manage to –

Linda   Never mind, Mam. Mam, isn't it great; if he's workin' an' we've got our own place he'll be able to get himself together an stop takin' those friggin' things . . .

They start to leave.

Mrs Johnstone   But, listen, Linda, who –

Linda   Oh, just some . . . some feller I know. He's . . . he's on the housin' committee. You don't know him, Mam . . .

Mrs Johnstone *exits.*

Mickey *and* **Linda** *are in their new house. In the lounge* **Linda** *is preparing* **Mickey***'s working things.*

Linda (*shouting*)   Mickey, Mickey, come on, you'll be late . . .

Mickey *enters his house.*

Mickey   Where's me . . .

Linda   Here . . . here's y' bag. Y' sandwiches are in there.

He ignores the bag and begins looking through a cupboard drawer.

Mickey, what y' lookin' for?

Mickey   Y' know what I'm lookin' for.

Linda   Mickey, Mickey, listen to me . . .

Mickey   Where's me tablets gone, Linda?

Linda   Mickey, you don't need your tablets!

Mickey   Linda!

Linda   Mickey, you're workin' now, we're livin' on our own – you've got to start makin' an effort.

Mickey   Give them to me, Linda.

Linda   You promised.

Mickey   I know I promised but I can't do without them. I tried. Last week I tried to do without them. By dinner time I was shakin' an' sweatin' so much I couldn't even work. I need them. That's all there is to it. Now give.

Pause.

Linda   Is that it then? Are y' gonna stay on them for ever?

Mickey   Linda.

Linda   Look . . . we've managed to sort ourselves out this far but what's the use if −

Mickey   *We* sorted ourselves out? Do you think I'm really stupid?

Linda   What?

Mickey   I didn't sort anythin' out, Linda. Not a job, not a house, nothin'. It used to be just sweets an' ciggies he gave me, because I had none of me own. Now it's a job and a house. I'm not stupid, Linda. You sorted it out. You an' Councillor Eddie Lyons.

Linda *doesn't deny it.*

Mickey   Now give me the tablets . . . I need them.

Linda   An' what about what I need? I need you. I love you. But, Mickey, not when you've got them inside you. When you take those things, Mickey, I can't even see you.

Mickey   That's why I take them. So I can be invisible.

Pause.

Now give me them.

Music. We see **Linda** *hand* **Mickey** *her bag.*

Mickey *quickly grabs the tablets.*

He exits.

The **Narrator** *enters.*

The **Narrator** *watches* **Linda**. *She moves to telephone, but hesitates.*

Narrator
>   There's a girl inside the woman
>   Who's waiting to get free
>   She's washed a million dishes
>   She's always making tea.

Linda (*speaking on the phone*)   Could I talk to Councillor Lyons, please?

Narrator
>   There's a girl inside the woman
>   And the mother she became
>   And a half-remembered song
>   Comes to her lips again.

Linda (*on the phone*)   Eddie, could I talk to you? Yeh, I remember.

Narrator
>   The girl would sing the melody
>   But the woman stands in doubt
>   And wonders what the price would be
>   For letting the young girl out.

Mrs Johnstone *enters.*

Mrs Johnstone (*singing*)
>   It's just a light romance,
>   It's nothing cruel,
>   They laid no plans,
>   How it came,
>   Who can explain?

Linda *approaches* **Edward** *who is waiting at the park fence.*

Mrs Johnstone (*singing*)
>   They just said 'hello',
>   And foolishly they gazed,
>   They should have gone
>   Their separate ways.

The music continues.

Edward   Hey. (*He mimes firing a gun.*)

Linda   Missed.

Edward *laughs, grabbing* **Linda** *jokingly. Their smiles fade as they look at each other. Suddenly they kiss. They walk together, hand in hand. All this through the following verse.*

Mrs Johnstone (*singing*)
    It's just the same old song,
    Nothing cruel,
    Nothing wrong.
    It's just two fools,
    Who know the rules,
    But break them all,
    And grasp at half a chance
    To play their part
    In a light romance.

Throughout the following chorus we see **Mickey** *at work. We see him go to take his pills. We see him make the effort of not taking them. We see the strain of this upon him but see that he is determined.*

Mrs Johnstone
    Living on the never never,
    Constant as the changing weather,
    Never sure
    Who's at the door,
    Or the price
    You're gonna have to pay.

We see **Linda** *and* **Edward** *kicking up the leaves before parting.*

Mrs Johnstone
    It's just a secret glance,
    Across a room.
    A touch of hands
    That part too soon.
    That same old tune
    That always plays,
    And lets them dance as friends,
    Then stand apart,
    As the music ends.

During the next chorus **Edward** *and* **Linda** *wave goodbye, as* **Edward** *and* **Mickey** *once did.*

Mrs Lyons *enters and goes to* **Mickey**.

She turns **Mickey** *round and points out* **Edward** *and* **Linda** *to him. By the end of the chorus* **Mickey** *is hammering on his own door.*

Mrs Johnstone
      Living on the never never,
      Constant as the changing weather,
      Never sure
      Who's at the door
      Or the price you're gonna have to pay.

As the music abruptly segues, **Mickey** *is heard hammering on his door and calling for* **Linda***, as he once did for his mother. The music pulsates and builds as he runs to his mother's house. He enters and flings back the floorboard to reveal the gun hidden by* **Sammy**.

Mrs Johnstone *enters just as* **Mickey** *disappears with the gun.*

Mrs Johnstone (*screaming*)   Mickey . . . Mickey . . .

We see **Mickey** *comb the town, breaking through groups of people, looking, searching, desperate, not even knowing what he's looking for or what he is going to do. His mother is frantically trying to catch him but not succeeding.*

Narrator
      There's a man gone mad in the town tonight,
      He's gonna shoot somebody down,
      There's a man gone mad, lost his mind tonight,
      There's a mad man
      There's a mad man
      There's a mad man running round and round.

      Now you know the devil's got your number,
      He's runnin' right beside you,
      He's screamin' deep inside you,
      And someone said he's callin' your number up today.

As **Mrs Johnstone** *makes her way to* **Linda***'s house.*

Narrator
There's a mad man / There's a mad man / There's a mad
man.

Mrs Johnstone *hammers on* **Linda***'s door, shouting her name.*
Linda*, just returning home, comes up behind her.*

Linda   Mam . . . Mam . . . what's . . .

Mrs Johnstone (*out of breath*)   He's . . . Mickey . . . Mickey's
got gun . . .

Linda   Mickey? . . . Eddie? . . . The Town Hall . . .

Mrs Johnstone   What?

Linda (*beginning to run*)   Eddie Lyons!

Narrator
There's a mad man running round and round
You know the devil's got your number
You know he's right beside you
He's screamin' deep inside you
And someone said he's callin' your number up today
Today
Today
TODAY!

On the last three words of the chorus **Mrs Johnstone** *runs off.*

On the last 'Today' the music stops abruptly.

We see **Edward***, standing behind a table, on a platform.*

*He is in the middle of addressing his audience. Two councillors stand
either side.*

Edward   And if, for once, I agree with Councillor Smith,
you mustn't hold that against me. But in this particular
instance, yes, I do agree with him. You're right, Bob, there is a
light at the end of the tunnel. Quite right. None of us would
argue with you on that score. But what we would question is
this, how many of us . . .

From his audience a commotion beginning. He thinks he is being heckled and so tries to carry on. In fact his audience is reacting to the sight of **Mickey** *appearing from the stalls, a gun held two-handed, to steady his shaking hands, and pointed directly at* **Edward**. **Edward** *turns and sees* **Mickey** *as someone on the platform next to him realises the reality of the situation and screams.*

Mickey   Stay where you are!

Mickey *stops a couple of yards from* **Edward**. *He's unsteady and breathing awkwardly.*

Edward (*eventually*)   Hello, Mickey.

Mickey   I stopped takin' the pills.

Edward (*pause*)   Oh.

Mickey (*eventually*)   I began thinkin' again. Y' see. (*To the councillors.*) Just get her out of here, mister, now!

The councillors hurry off.

Edward *and* **Mickey** *are now alone on the platform.*

Mickey   I had to start thinkin' again. Because there was one thing left in my life. (*Pause.*) Just one thing I had left, Eddie – Linda – an' I wanted to keep her. So, so I stopped takin' the pills. But it was too late. D' y' know who told me about . . . you . . . an' Linda . . . your mother . . . she came to the factory and told me.

Edward   Mickey, I don't know what she told you, but Linda and I are just friends . . .

Mickey (*shouting for the first time*)   Friends! I could kill you. We were friends, weren't we? Blood brothers, wasn't it? Remember?

Edward   Yes, Mickey, I remember.

Mickey   Well, how come you got everything . . . an' I got nothin'? (*Pause.*) Friends. I've been thinkin' again, Eddie. You an' Linda were friends when she first got pregnant, weren't y'?

Edward   Mickey!

Mickey   Does my child belong to you as well as everythin' else? Does she, Eddie, does she?

Edward (*shouting*)   No, for God's sake!

Pause.

From the back of the auditorium we hear a **Policeman** *through a loudhailer.*

Policeman 1   Now listen, son, listen to me, I've got armed marksmen with me. But if you do exactly as I say we won't need to use them, will we? Now look, Michael, put down the gun, just put the gun down, son.

Mickey (*dismissing their presence*)   What am I doin' here, Eddie? I thought I was gonna shoot y'. But I can't even do that. I don't even know if the thing's loaded.

Mrs Johnstone *slowly walks down the centre aisle towards the platform.*

Policeman 2   What's that woman doin'?

Policeman 1   Get that woman away . . .

Policeman 2   Oh Christ.

Mrs Johnstone   Mickey. Mickey. Don't shoot him, Mickey . . .

Mickey *continues to hold the gun in position.*

Mickey   Go away, Mam . . . Mam, you go away from here.

Mrs Johnstone   No, son. (*She walks on to the platform.*)

Mickey (*shouting*)   Mam!

Mrs Johnstone   Mickey. Don't shoot Eddie. He's your brother. You had a twin brother. I couldn't afford to keep both of you. His mother couldn't have kids. I agreed to give one of you away!

Mickey (*something that begins deep down inside him*)   You! (*Screaming.*) You! Why didn't you give me away? (*He stands glaring at her, almost uncontrollable with rage.*) I could have been . . . I could have been him!

On the word 'him' **Mickey** *waves at* **Edward** *with his gun hand.*
The gun explodes and blows **Edward** *apart.* **Mickey** *turns to the*
Policemen*, screaming the word 'No'. They open fire and four guns*
explode, blowing **Mickey** *away.* **Linda** *runs down the aisle.*

The **Policemen** *are heard through the loudhailer.*

Policemen   Nobody move, please. It's all right, it's all over,
just stay where you are.

Music.

As the light on the scene begins to dim we see the **Narrator** *watching.*

Narrator
And do we blame superstition for what came to pass?
Or could it be what we, the English, have come to know
     as class?
Did you ever hear the story of the Johnstone twins,
As like each other as two new pins,
How one was kept and one given away,
How they were born, and they died, on the selfsame day?

Mrs Johnstone (*singing*)
Tell me it's not true,
Say it's just a story.
Something on the news.
Tell me it's not true.
Though it's here before me,
Say it's just a dream,
Say it's just a scene
From an old movie of years ago,
From an old movie of Marilyn Monroe.

Say it's just some clowns,
Two players in the limelight,
And bring the curtain down.
Say it's just two clowns,
Who couldn't get their lines right,
Say it's just a show
On the radio,
That we can turn over and start again,
That we can turn over; it's only a game.

Company
    Tell me it's not true,
    Say I only dreamed it,
    And morning will come soon,
    Tell me it's not true,
    Say you didn't mean it,
    Say it's just pretend,
    Say it's just the end
    Of an old movie from years ago
    Of an old movie with Marilyn Monroe.

Curtain.

Methuen Drama Student Editions

Jean Anouilh *Antigone* • John Arden *Serjeant Musgrave's Dance*
Alan Ayckbourn *Confusions* • Aphra Behn *The Rover* • Edward Bond
Lear • *Saved* • Bertolt Brecht *The Caucasian Chalk Circle* • *Fear and
Misery in the Third Reich* • *The Good Person of Szechwan* • *Life of Galileo* •
Mother Courage and her Children• *The Resistible Rise of Arturo Ui* • *The
Threepenny Opera* • Anton Chekhov *The Cherry Orchard* • *The Seagull* •
Three Sisters • *Uncle Vanya* • Caryl Churchill *Serious Money* • *Top Girls*
• Shelagh Delaney *A Taste of Honey* • Euripides *Elektra* • *Medea*•
Dario Fo *Accidental Death of an Anarchist* • Michael Frayn *Copenhagen*
• John Galsworthy *Strife* • Nikolai Gogol *The Government Inspector* •
Robert Holman *Across Oka* • Henrik Ibsen *A Doll's House* • *Ghosts*•
Hedda Gabler • Charlotte Keatley *My Mother Said I Never Should* •
Bernard Kops *Dreams of Anne Frank* • Federico García Lorca *Blood
Wedding* • *Doña Rosita the Spinster* (bilingual edition) •*The House of
Bernarda Alba* • (bilingual edition) • *Yerma* (bilingual edition) • David
Mamet *Glengarry Glen Ross* • *Oleanna* • Patrick Marber *Closer* • John
Marston *Malcontent* • Martin McDonagh *The Lieutenant of Inishmore* •
Joe Orton *Loot* • Luigi Pirandello *Six Characters in Search of an Author*
• Mark Ravenhill *Shopping and F***ing* • Willy Russell *Blood Brothers*
• *Educating Rita* • Sophocles *Antigone* • *Oedipus the King* • Wole
Soyinka *Death and the King's Horseman* • Shelagh Stephenson *The
Memory of Water* • August Strindberg *Miss Julie* • J. M. Synge *The
Playboy of the Western World* • Theatre Workshop *Oh What a Lovely
War* Timberlake Wertenbaker *Our Country's Good* • Arnold Wesker
The Merchant • Oscar Wilde *The Importance of Being Earnest* •
Tennessee Williams *A Streetcar Named Desire* • *The Glass Menagerie*

Methuen Drama Modern Classics

Jean Anouilh *Antigone* • Brendan Behan *The Hostage* • Robert Bolt
A Man for All Seasons • Edward Bond *Saved* • Bertolt Brecht *The
Caucasian Chalk Circle* • *Fear and Misery in the Third Reich* • *The Good
Person of Szechwan* • *Life of Galileo* • *The Messingkauf Dialogues* •
Mother Courage and Her Children • *Mr Puntila and His Man Matti* •
The Resistible Rise of Arturo Ui • *Rise and Fall of the City of
Mahagonny* • *The Threepenny Opera* • Jim Cartwright *Road* • *Two &
Bed* • Caryl Churchill *Serious Money* • *Top Girls* • Noël Coward
Blithe Spirit • *Hay Fever* • *Present Laughter* • *Private Lives* • *The Vortex* •
Shelagh Delaney *A Taste of Honey* • Dario Fo *Accidental Death of an
Anarchist* • Michael Frayn *Copenhagen* • Lorraine Hansberry *A
Raisin in the Sun* • Jonathan Harvey *Beautiful Thing* • David Mamet
Glengarry Glen Ross • *Oleanna* • *Speed-the-Plow* • Patrick Marber
Closer • *Dealer's Choice* • Arthur Miller *Broken Glass* • Percy Mtwa,
Mbongeni Ngema, Barney Simon *Woza Albert!* • Joe Orton
Entertaining Mr Sloane • *Loot* • *What the Butler Saw* • Mark Ravenhill
*Shopping and F***ing* • Willy Russell *Blood Brothers* • *Educating Rita* •
Stags and Hens • *Our Day Out* • Jean-Paul Sartre *Crime Passionnel* •
Wole Soyinka • *Death and the King's Horseman* • Theatre Workshop
Oh, What a Lovely War • Frank Wedekind • *Spring Awakening* •
Timberlake Wertenbaker *Our Country's Good*

Methuen Drama Contemporary Dramatists

include

John Arden (two volumes)
Arden & D'Arcy
Peter Barnes (three volumes)
Sebastian Barry
Dermot Bolger
Edward Bond (eight volumes)
Howard Brenton
  (two volumes)
Richard Cameron
Jim Cartwright
Caryl Churchill (two volumes)
Sarah Daniels (two volumes)
Nick Darke
David Edgar (three volumes)
David Eldridge
Ben Elton
Dario Fo (two volumes)
Michael Frayn (three volumes)
David Greig
John Godber (four volumes)
Paul Godfrey
John Guare
Lee Hall (two volumes)
Peter Handke
Jonathan Harvey
  (two volumes)
Declan Hughes
Terry Johnson (three volumes)
Sarah Kane
Barrie Keeffe
Bernard-Marie Koltès
  (two volumes)
Franz Xaver Kroetz
David Lan
Bryony Lavery
Deborah Levy
Doug Lucie

David Mamet (four volumes)
Martin McDonagh
Duncan McLean
Anthony Minghella
  (two volumes)
Tom Murphy (six volumes)
Phyllis Nagy
Anthony Neilsen (two volumes)
Philip Osment
Gary Owen
Louise Page
Stewart Parker (two volumes)
Joe Penhall (two volumes)
Stephen Poliakoff
  (three volumes)
David Rabe (two volumes)
Mark Ravenhill (two volumes)
Christina Reid
Philip Ridley
Willy Russell
Eric-Emmanuel Schmitt
Ntozake Shange
Sam Shepard (two volumes)
Wole Soyinka (two volumes)
Simon Stephens (two volumes)
Shelagh Stephenson
David Storey (three volumes)
Sue Townsend
Judy Upton
Michel Vinaver
  (two volumes)
Arnold Wesker (two volumes)
Michael Wilcox
Roy Williams (three volumes)
Snoo Wilson (two volumes)
David Wood (two volumes)
Victoria Wood

Methuen Drama World Classics

include

Jean Anouilh (two volumes)
Brendan Behan
Aphra Behn
Bertolt Brecht (eight volumes)
Büchner
Bulgakov
Calderón
Čapek
Anton Chekhov
Noël Coward (eight volumes)
Feydeau (two volumes)
Eduardo De Filippo
Max Frisch
John Galsworthy
Gogol
Gorky (two volumes)
Harley Granville Barker
  (two volumes)
Victor Hugo
Henrik Ibsen (six volumes)
Jarry

Lorca (three volumes)
Marivaux
Mustapha Matura
David Mercer (two volumes)
Arthur Miller (six volumes)
Molière
Musset
Peter Nichols (two volumes)
Joe Orton
A. W. Pinero
Luigi Pirandello
Terence Rattigan
  (two volumes)
W. Somerset Maugham
  (two volumes)
August Strindberg
  (three volumes)
J. M. Synge
Ramón del Valle-Inclán
Frank Wedekind
Oscar Wilde

Methuen Drama Classical Greek Dramatists

Aeschylus Plays: One
(Persians, Seven Against Thebes, Suppliants,
Prometheus Bound)

Aeschylus Plays: Two
(Oresteia: Agamemnon, Libation-Bearers, Eumenides)

Aristophanes Plays: One
(Acharnians, Knights, Peace, Lysistrata)

Aristophanes Plays: Two
(Wasps, Clouds, Birds, Festival Time, Frogs)

Aristophanes & Menander: New Comedy
(Women in Power, Wealth, The Malcontent,
The Woman from Samos)

Euripides Plays: One
(Medea, The Phoenician Women, Bacchae)

Euripides Plays: Two
(Hecuba, The Women of Troy, Iphigeneia at Aulis,
Cyclops)

Euripides Plays: Three
(Alkestis, Helen, Ion)

Euripides Plays: Four
(Elektra, Orestes, Iphigeneia in Tauris)

Euripides Plays: Five
(Andromache, Herakles' Children, Herakles)

Euripides Plays: Six
(Hippolytos, Suppliants, Rhesos)

Sophocles Plays: One
(Oedipus the King, Oedipus at Colonus, Antigone)

Sophocles Plays: Two
(Ajax, Women of Trachis, Electra, Philoctetes)

For a complete catalogue
of Methuen Drama titles
write to:

Methuen Drama
36 Soho Square
London W1D 3QY

or you can visit our website at:

www.methuendrama.com